The Animal Contract

Books by Desmond Morris

The Naked Ape
The Human Zoo
Intimate Behaviour
Manwatching
Gestures
The Soccer Tribe
Bodywatching
Animal Days
The Book of Ages
Dogwatching
Catwatching
Catlore
Horsewatching
The Animal Contract

The Animal Contract,

Sharing the Planet

based on the television series

by

Desmond Morris

VIRGIN

For GEORGE COURI and ROBERT PAGE

without whose encouragement this book would not have grown out of the television series, and my special thanks also to Christine Townend for valuable discussions, Serena Dilnot for her painstaking editorial assistance, and Stafford Garner for his patience when directing me during location filming.

First published in Great Britain in 1990 by
Virgin Books
A division of W.H. Allen & Co Plc
Sekforde House
175–9 St John Street
London EC1V 4LL

British Library Cataloguing in Publication Data
Morris, Desmond. *1928–*
    The animal contract.
    1. Man. Relationships with animals. 2. Animals.
    Relationships with man
    I. Title
    304.2

ISBN 1–85227–392–5

Set in Sabon by Phoenix Photosetting, Chatham, Kent

Printed and bound in Great Britain by
Butler & Tanner Ltd, Frome & London

Contents

Foreword

For some years I have felt the need to make a personal statement about the way our species has been behaving towards other animals; the way human beings have repeatedly abused and exploited the animal kingdom. This was not easy for me because I have never been a campaigner or a crusader. All I ever wanted to do with animals was to watch them and try to understand them. I argued that if, through books and television programmes, I could show animals to be fascinating and enjoyable, people would come to respect them and, like me, would want to become observers rather than manipulators or persecutors. I thought that would be enough, but recently I came to the conclusion that something extra was necessary.

The abuses still remain. There is much more concern now, it is true, but animals still suffer in a hundred different ways. However, I did not want to join one of the campaigning groups, partly because I am not by nature a joiner and partly because I could never find a group that matched precisely my own viewpoint. All too often animal welfare crusaders, despite their good intentions, allow themselves to become over-emotional when what is needed is a cool head. They become obsessed with narrower issues when what is required is an attack on major principles of human conduct. All too often it is the horrific effects of animal abuses that are being tackled instead of the primary causes.

I became convinced that what was necessary was a new Bill of Rights for animals, and I was fortunate enough to be approached in 1988 by a television company that wanted to make a series on this very subject. I travelled to all five continents to make these programmes and was able to see at first hand many of the problems that beset animals today. This small book is a modified and extended version of the scripts I wrote for that series. It is not intended to be a comprehensive report on the subject: that would inevitably become a huge volume and would probably never be read. Instead this short presentation of my ideas and thoughts on the subject of mankind's relationship with other species is easy to digest, even if by following the scripts rather closely it must omit a great deal of this vast topic. For that I apologise, but sometimes a brief message is heard when a longer one is ignored.

Desmond Morris

Oxford, 1990

Introduction

At the last count there were 5000 million human beings swarming over the surface of this small planet. Not so long ago, in the Stone Age, we had only a fragile foothold on it. Then we spread out, multiplying our numbers until now we have become an infestation. The changes we have wrought on our environment are rapidly making the planet unfit for human habitation. We are victims of our own ingenuity. That ingenuity will result in our already massive population doubling to 10,000 million in less than 40 years. Rare we are not, but an endangered species we are.

We are faced with nothing short of a problem of survival, but it is easy to hide from this fact. There are still places in the world where it is possible to be seduced into believing that all is well. In parts of Africa, for example, where the air is clear and fresh, and the wild game appears untroubled, open spaces stretch as far as the eye can see: nature seems to be at peace with itself. Appearances can be deceptive.

Man is encroaching on the wild spaces at such a rate that within only two generations they could simply have ceased to exist. The question we should all be asking ourselves is, need this be so? Is the crash inevitable? Have we simply broken too many rules?

Environmentalists are increasingly preoccupied with the way we are polluting the waters, laying waste the land and corrupting the atmosphere, but there is another crime that humanity is committing against itself: the breaking of the Animal Contract. This is the contract that exists between ourselves and the other animals, making us partners in sharing the planet.

The basis of this contract is that each species must limit its population growth sufficiently to permit other life forms to coexist with it. There is competition, of course, but it is not as ruthless as some people seem to imagine. Any species that competes so savagely that it wipes out everything else has won a hollow victory: what it now dominates is nothing but a wasteland, and wastelands do not sustain life forms, even dominant ones.

Other animals have managed to honour their contracts with one another and we must learn from them. If well-fed lions were to roam the plains of Africa killing every available zebra and antelope, simply because they are strong enough and fast enough to do so, their prey would quickly become extinct, and the lions themselves would then perish. All forms of life are interdependent. Predators need prey and prey need vegetation. Overpopulation means famine and each species has evolved its own form of population control that prevents its numbers rising to a disaster level. A common form of control is one in which the females cease to breed when overcrowded. Their embryos may fail to develop, or the mothers may fail to rear their young after they have been born. This reduces the population to a level at which it can once again start to breed, and normal reproduction is resumed.

Our ancient ancestors must have had some sort of population control mechanism of their own, but it clearly was not based on overcrowding. For a million years or so our early forebears lived in small tribes of perhaps 80–100 individuals. Hunting for meat became their special way of living and as long as there was plenty of space they thrived. It was probably availability of food that acted as their particular population control system. With the whole of the earth's surface to spread into, overcrowding was not a problem and could not have started to operate as a control mechanism.

If we had increased our numbers very gradually, we would undoubtedly have evolved the kind of population control that we see in other species, but we did not. Because of our ingenuity and our sudden technological advances, our numbers exploded. In 10,000 years – a mere drop in the evolutionary ocean of time – we advanced from the Stone Age to the Nuclear Age, carrying with us our tribal genetic legacy. It was a legacy that said, if you have food, breed as much as you like. Our technology made our population control mechanism ineffectual and we had no time to acquire a new biological brake that could be applied as our numbers soared.

The result was that we started to rape the planet, a process that we confused with progress. To have progressed appropriately we should have concentrated on quality rather than quantity: our numbers would have risen steadily and the quality of life would have risen with them. Instead, we have seen the opposite occur. The quality of life for some may be better than ever, but for countless millions the daily grind is worse than it was back in those affluent, tribal hunting days of the Stone Age. The faster their numbers have risen, the worse has been their lot.

Apart from the damage to our physical environment, our headlong rush to world domination has isolated our species from the important basic truth that we are animals and part of

11

an interacting biosphere. We have exploited exciting new innovations without considering their possible drawbacks. Human inventiveness has been like a drug we have failed to test for side-effects. We have dragged our primeval bodies behind us into an amazing, futuristic playground, full of diverting delights. We have dazzled ourselves and even, occasionally, contemplated the possibility that we are not animals after all, but gods. As such, of course, we would be immune from the hazards of natural laws, protected by our sacred status.

The folly of this delusion is already being glimpsed, at least in some of the more enlightened parts of the world. The awful thought that we could wake up one morning and find the planet irreversibly wrecked has started to seep into our consciousness. How can we have let this happen? The answer, it seems to me, is that it all began when we broke the Animal Contract: as soon as we started to overpower our animal companions, we were in trouble. We began to create an increasingly one-sided world, full of basic instabilities that even our great ingenuity could not control. In 10,000 years we have upset the balance of nature to such an extent that it will now take a major shift in human thinking to correct the damage.

The breaking of the Animal Contract has been damaging in two distinct ways. In the first place, it has disrupted the complex biological network of life forms on this planet. This has been unsettled and distorted to such a degree that there are now serious risks of food crises, famine, epidemics, and a breakdown in vegetation cycles. We may turn out to be the greatest desert-builders in the history of the planet.

In addition, it has made us so remote from our animal companions that we no longer think in a biological way. We no longer realise that we need biological solutions to many of our problems: not chemical ones, or mathematical ones, or even political ones, but animal solutions because we ourselves are animals. To understand this we need to have as close a rapport as possible with other species. The terms of the contracts under which we share the planet with them should be based on respect rather than exploitation. We must stop breaking the Animal Contract and restrain our urge to dominate all other species out of existence.

We need to examine dispassionately and coolly the errors we have made, and how and why we have made them. All too often when examining our deteriorating relations with other animals we have resorted to emotional pleas. It is easy to see why we have done this, but such pleas are less helpful than they may at first appear. When a judge considers the breaking of a human law, he does so calmly and carefully. When we consider the breaking of a natural law, we too must act like judges. Before we pass sentence on our species we must consider the facts. What is the full story of the Animal Contract? How did it begin, when our species was young, and how has it been broken in the eras that followed? Can we, from studying this, find a way of repairing the contract before it is too late? These are the questions we must now set out to answer.

I

The Company of Animals

The Company of Animals

In the days when superstition dominated reason and magical powers suppressed common sense, animal spirits infested the world of our ancestors. Endowed with supernatural qualities like our own, the animals we encountered filled us with awe. We tried to control them with the aid of ritual dances and ceremonies, often building myths and legends out of mimed animal dramas. For some tribal groups surviving today, this myth-making process continues, and is a vivid reminder of a vision of animals once common to the whole of mankind. Animals were transformed into forces of good and evil. We worshipped the good and feared the evil, attempting to placate both with outlandish rituals and occult ceremonies.

Our reverence for our animal companions began far back in prehistoric times. We do not know the precise moment when we first viewed them imaginatively as our soul brothers, but we can be certain that it dates from before the Old Stone Age 20,000 years ago. By then the process was already at a remarkably advanced, sophisticated stage, as a visit to the painted caves of France and Spain will testify.

Nearby these caves our forebears lived as hunters: hunters who respected their prey. They had good reason to do so, for the wild bulls, mammoths, woolly rhino and wild boar they hunted were formidable adversaries. The hunting tribes never regarded these other animals as their inferiors. Indeed, they undoubtedly noticed that in many respects – muscular strength, speed, hearing, sense of smell – they were superior to humans. When fear of death led us to the concept of an afterlife, it was natural to endow our animal companions with the same spirituality that we bestowed upon ourselves. If we had souls, then so did they.

We have proof of this on the walls of the painted caves, where our ancestors have left us an amazing legacy: the carefully fashioned images of their prey. These are not casual sketches, roughly drawn as instructional guides for apprentice hunters. They are, by the standards of any age, works of art; images made special by the care lavished on them. Bearing in mind the crude technology available to the Stone Age artists – the poor illumination, the restricted pigments and the simplicity of the implements – the aesthetic skill they demonstrate is astonishing. What drove these early hunters to such peaks of achievement?

For many years it was thought that the primary motive was sympathetic magic: the act of painting a living bull on the cave wall would give power over it. By performing some killing ritual in the cave in which the image was symbolically speared to death, spearing the real bull would be made easier.

This was a good guess but it now appears to have been a mistaken one. If the images are examined with a zoologist's eye, something new emerges: they are accurately portrayed not in life, but in postures of death. The clue comes in the feet, and is a clue that has been missed by most of the observers that have studied them. The position of the hooves reveals that the weight of the animals is exerting no pressure upon them. These are the feet of dead animals lying on their sides rather than, as has nearly always been claimed, standing up: the paintings are precise, commemorative studies of freshly killed prey.

The artists must have made careful sketches in the field, copying with great dexterity the attitudes of death and then returning with these sketches to the safety of the caves to capture the moment permanently on the rocky surfaces. The finished pictures are memorials which involved a major effort, reflecting a huge respect for the spirits of the animals slain. These were spirits that had to be appeased by the enshrinement of their images deep in the safest places known to these early hunters. The body of the prey would be eaten, its bones turned into tools and its skin worn as clothes, but its soul would still have a home in the painted and engraved form: the more skilfully the artists depicted the shapes and details of the prey, the more readily would their spirits take to their new abodes.

Significantly, only the most dangerous and impressive of the prey species were commonly depicted. Cattle, horses, mammoths, rhino, ibex, deer, bison and wild boar are the animals most frequently recorded. The smaller animals, which we know (from the debris of the cave floors) were eaten in large numbers, are rarely, if ever, shown. Apparently we did not fear them enough. Their small, harmless souls were not worth the trouble of appeasement.

This selectivity, showing great respect for some species but little for others, was the weakness of the early Animal Contract based on the idea that animals had souls. Because the souls were an imaginative invention they were susceptible to the whims of the inventors. There was no generalised awe for animal life, but rather an awe related to whichever animals were chosen as spiritually significant. As time passed this led to a curious bias that saw certain animals chosen by particular tribes as their own personal soul brothers, or totems.

Each totemic animal eventually became so revered that it was no longer hunted. To kill it became strictly taboo. It was now considered sacred and its flesh could not be eaten. It was protected because it was believed to have a special relationship with the tribespeople. To some it was an ancestral figure, from which they themselves had descended. This is a primitive form of evolutionary thinking which clearly placed man and animal in an intimate relation with one another. To others it was the vehicle for reincarnation when they themselves died. To others again it was a great creator, a sacred scout, a guide for the soul on its journey to the afterlife, a messenger of the gods, or even the god itself.

Animal totems of this kind were widespread in tribal society and they formed the background against which more complex forms of animal worship was to develop in the earliest civilisations. Nowhere was this more abundantly displayed than in ancient Egypt, where animals played a major role in human thought.

The Egyptians' obsession with animals of many kinds kept them closely involved with non-human species. It is clear from the detail and beauty of their many skilful paintings, carvings and sculptures of animal forms that the inhabitants of this early civilisation were genuinely fascinated by their richly varied companions. The Egyptians paid close attention to everything from dung-beetles to hippos, from scorpions to leopards, from frogs to mongooses. In many cases they kept them, tamed them and attempted to domesticate them. They did more in this respect than any other culture at that time, and their intimacy with animals created an atmosphere in which a true sense of wonder for the natural world could blossom.

It would be a mistake, however, if we were to gaze at the Egyptians' animal images as if we were examining natural history illustrations. They are much more than that, for to the ancient Egyptians a statue or a carving possessed the same powers as the subject it portrayed. An image of an animal was itself the animal.

For instance, at the great temple complex of Karnak near present-day Luxor, there is an impressive avenue lined with ram-headed sphinxes. They guard the processional way down which the king would have walked, and would have given him a sense of power and protection. By combining the heads of rams (symbols of sexuality) with the bodies of lions (symbols of massive strength), it was possible to create an imaginary hybrid creature that could give the king a feeling of both virility and security.

As the king walked down his huge avenue he would have felt the impact of these stone images so intensely that his whole mood would have been transformed. This was the secret of holy places, of sacred temples and revered sanctuaries. Today we marvel at the architectural feats and the decorative artwork, but these are really secondary considerations. At the very core of the ancient centres is the magical property of the images depicted there. The Egyptians believed that these effigies, once completed, existed as real forces and could exert real influence over human affairs. The animals shown there were more than natural animals: they were super-animals with supernatural powers.

Where the forms depicted happened to be terrifying, the atmosphere of the temples must have been full of fear and dread. The temple of Mut, full of huge stone figures of the lion-headed goddess Sekhmet, is such a place. Sekhmet was the most bloodthirsty of all the ancient deities. She spread terror wherever she went and the burning desert winds were said to be nothing less than her fiery breath.

Lions were common in ancient Egypt and often preyed upon domestic animals at the edge of the Nile. This was the source of the fear they aroused and explains their role as a savage, devouring deity. As the Goddess of War, Sekhmet was believed to accompany the king into battle and enable him to slaughter his enemies without mercy. An old legend tells how, because she was so bloodthirsty, she could be defeated only by a clever trick. She loved nothing more than drinking the blood that flooded the battlefields, so it was possible to render her insensible by dyeing beer red and then pouring it over the fields. After she had lapped it all up she was too drunk to continue her reign of terror.

Sekhmet was so adept at killing the king's enemies that she inevitably became a great protectress. Evil spirits that caused sickness were also the king's enemies, so they too could be attacked by her. As a result, the Goddess of War was also a Mistress of Healing. Such were the twists in animal roles, in ancient Egyptian thinking.

A further twist was to come when the smaller wild cat of Egypt was domesticated as a pest-destroyer. As the protector of the grain-stores this cat became crucially important to Egyptian civilisation and was soon one of the most revered and protected of species. This meant that Sekhmet had to be tamed and transformed, the early, ferocious feline deity being converted into the smaller, more lovable one. In this way feline magic could persist, but in a new context.

The new cat goddess was known as Bastet. Paradoxically she was both a virgin goddess and a mother, making her the forerunner of Christianity's Virgin Mary. Annual festivals were held in her honour and attracted bigger crowds than any other festive gathering in ancient Egypt, largely because there was orgiastic worshipping, accompanied by ritual frenzies and a vast consumption of wine. Massive gatherings of 700,000 people were reported, although this was doubtless an exaggeration.

On some of the images of Bastet it is possible to detect a beetle engraved between the ears, or on the chest. There is no zoological explanation for this association. Cats and beetles have no biological connection. To understand this strange animal conjunction it is necessary to think like the ancient Egyptians for a moment. To them, the fertilising power of the sun was all-important. The intense sexuality of the cat, with its lascivious mating activities, made it a symbol of fertility: hence it was connected with the sun. The rolling of a ball of dung by the dung-beetle was seen as the symbolic rolling of the solar ball through the heavens: the beetle was also connected with the sun. Both cat and beetle were agents of the mighty sun-god and so were depicted together.

Anyone approaching Egyptian art or religion for the first time is likely to find the multiplicity of the animal gods bewildering. The legends surrounding them are confusing and often contradictory. Deities change from one form into another, and split or amalgamate without any apparent reason. Sometimes a particular god takes animal form, then half-animal half-human, then completely human. How can one make any sense out of it all, and what does this tell us about the Egyptian attitude to real animals?

The explanation lies in Egypt's strange geography. Despite its rectangular outline on a map, Egypt is in reality a long narrow country surrounded by barren desert. A thin, fertile strip of land flanks the River Nile, and it was this land that eventually gave Egypt its agricultural strength as one of the first great civilised powers. However, being a country effectively 600 miles long and only a few miles wide created its own special problems. How could any ruling group control it and weld it into a single nation?

Initially there was no answer to this question. All along the banks of the Nile there were small prehistoric tribes, each with its own independent leaders and its own totemic animal god. At one centre the tribesmen were praying to a god in the form of a crocodile, at another an antelope, or a cat or a lion or a ram or a baboon. Each animal god had its own special name and its own rituals and ceremonies.

It was the need to organise efficient irrigation systems that provided the impetus for the strongest tribes to try to take control of the whole of the Nile. When they succeeded, it was their totem animals (especially the falcon and the ibis) that became the most widespread, replacing many of the others, and gaining a supra-tribal significance. The special geographical nature of Egypt meant that the whole region went straight from the primitive, tribal condition to that of cohesive ancient empire, without the usual intermediate conditions. As a result, the primitive and the advanced attitudes towards animals became muddled together, creating the menagerie of animal gods that we still see depicted on the walls of the country's huge monuments and in its decorated tombs.

During Egypt's growth from the tribal to the imperial, her totem animals went through three main phases of development. At first they were simple animals, revered and protected as ancestral tribal figures. If they were depicted as images, these took the form of the animal itself. Then, as time passed, the gods became humanised and grew human bodies, while still retaining their animal heads. Jackal- or ibis-headed humans, and others with the heads of falcons, crocodiles, lions, rams and cows are to be found in temple after temple. These strange amalgams probably stemmed from the ancient habit of humans dressing up as the totem animal and dancing in this disguise at special festivals and ceremonies. Masked dancers of this kind, wearing animal heads, are known from as long ago as the Old Stone Age and are still common today in many of the surviving tribal societies.

The next step, as primitive magical rituals gave way to more organised, recorded and institutionalised religious systems, was the complete humanisation of the gods. The animal heads were banished along with their bodies and the gods were shown in totally human form. The old totemic concepts were dying out, together with the small, tribal units. Animals did not disappear from religious ritual altogether. Instead they survived in the form of representatives of the gods. In this condition they were considered sacred and were still pro-tected, even though they were no longer seen as gods them-selves. When they died they were given full rites including embalming and were buried with due pomp and ritual. Literally millions of them were treated in this way.

This blending and mixing of animal and human shows how close the two were in the minds of the early thinkers. Animals were not yet reduced to the level of soulless inferiors. That was a degradation they would not suffer for many centuries. For the time being the relationship between humans and animals was one of spiritual equality. Animals were still mysterious and often dangerous, and in the minds of these early Egyptians they gave rise to fears and apprehensions that put them on a par with humans.

Despite this, there was a grave disadvantage to being a sacred animal. The chosen species might be pampered and even honoured in death; it might be a capital offence to harm them, as was the case in Egypt for cats, ibises and falcons. However, this adoration was based, not on their rights as animals or their qualities as sensitive biological phenomena, but on the belief that they were incarnations of some super-natural force. This belief was as unreliable as it was ill-founded.

If it was decided that one particular kind of animal was not sacred, then it could be treated as brutally as human whim dictated. If an animal happened to be the sacred totem of some hated rival culture, it could be attacked and destroyed at will. Even the sacred ones were not as safe as might be imagined. Recently, examination of the mummified remains of sacred animals has revealed that, far from dying of old age, they were young specimens, barely adult, and in each case had died from having the neck broken. Looking at the huge numbers involved in the embalming and burial ceremonies, it is clear that supplies from the wild could not have kept pace with demand. Once the religious rituals had become popular events, the priests or their servants must have established huge breeding colonies to provide the faithful with the necessary mummified bodies for temple offerings. Whether or not the general public knew what was going on is hard to say. Officially it was a crime to hurt one of these animals, but the priests somehow managed to organise the festivals without creating a scandal, killing and stuffing thousands of unfor-tunate cats, ibises and other creatures, as though they were modern turkey-farmers. Such are the risks of being the object of religious interest, as many a martyred saint was to discover.

Almost any significance could be placed upon any kind of animal by a sufficiently ingenious priesthood. Indeed, the artistic licence that exaggerates animal shapes for visual effect dwindles into insignificance beside religious licence. A sacred animal could magically become terrifying, friendly, huge, minute, godlike or fiendish, according to the completely fanciful whims of the legend-makers. Animals were not respected for themselves but for their symbolic qualities. If their visual portrayals are accurate, this has more to do with honouring them than representing them with zoological precision. Their depictions may be anatomically correct while at the same time standing for some quality that is totally alien to their real nature. The only redeeming feature of this nonsensical religious attitude towards animals is that it did elevate them – or at least some of them – to a high status.

Because of the oddity of thought involved in creating the animal gods of Egypt, certain animals, such as scorpions, frogs, jackals and vultures, that are disliked by most cultures, were viewed in an unexpectedly warm and friendly light. This applied in particular to snakes. Being venomous, snakes have been widely feared and hated as deadly enemies by mankind, but to ancient Egyptians they took on another, more glorious role. To them, the snake became a symbol of immortality, the most precious quality of which they could conceive.

The reason for this particular symbolism is not hard to find. When a snake sheds its skin it re-emerges into the world, glistening and new, as if reborn. To the superstitious mind this can mean only one thing: if you shed your skin like a snake, you are reborn. It has been suggested that it was this observation that led to the ancient Egyptian custom of circumcision, the shedding of the foreskin from the snakelike phallus supposedly giving the circumcised male a serpentine immortality. This curious custom of the Egyptians was later borrowed by both Jews and Muslims and persists to this day, a relic of the time when snakes were viewed with awe and reverence. In modern times, of course, these primitive origins of the ritual mutilation of the young have to be concealed and new reasons given for removing part of the penis. Completely spurious medical reasons are now offered to explain this bizarre operation. The ancient Egyptian snake connection has long been forgotten.

The snake took many forms in Egyptian mythology, as a great creator, as the guardian of the earth, as the spirit of the underworld, as a fertility spirit, and as a water god. As the serpent god Sito, Son of Earth, the snake was depicted encircling the world, protecting it from the cosmic forces that were constantly threatening it. The wonderfully decorated tombs in the Valley of the Kings are alive with snake images. One serpent is 36 feet long and walks on eight legs. Others undulate with many coils and wrap themselves around the depicted scenes. Still others spit fire from their mouths as they stride bipedally on stout limbs. Certain of the ancient texts even suggest that, in the very beginning, God himself took the form of a serpent and that when we have finally destroyed the world and reduced everything to chaos once more, he will again return to serpentine form. God the Snake is vividly described by the Egyptian scribes as 'that great surviving serpent, when all mankind has reverted to slime'.

This Egyptian obsession with snakes was bound to have repercussions. The immense popularity of serpent gods and goddesses inevitably meant that they had to suffer in later religions. For example, the great protective snake was cunningly transformed into the evil serpent in the Garden of Eden. This famous legend from the Book of Genesis was in reality a piece of coded history, a warning to neighbouring tribesmen that, if they enjoyed the fruits of the advanced knowledge of the already civilised Egyptians, they would feel naked and ashamed of their own simple way of life, and could easily be exploited. Seen in this way, the puzzling story of Adam and Eve begins to make sense. The serpent in the garden was Egypt – beguiling and seductive – enslaving the innocent Adam and Eve and condemning them to a life of toil. To outsiders, the serpent became a wicked animal and a symbol of evil.

Despite the fact that snakes are shy and retiring, never attack unless sorely provoked, and devour the rats and mice that are the pests of human settlements and farms, the snake has been severely persecuted, beyond all reason, largely as a result of this ancient association. Christians in particular hated the snake and believed that inside its slithering form it harboured their greatest enemy, the Devil himself.

This widespread attitude has crystallised in a dramatic form in the snake-handling cults of the United States. In churches rejoicing in such names as 'The Dolley Pond Church of God with Signs Following', 'The Full Gospel Jesus Church of Colombus' and 'The Church of Lord Jesus in Jolo West Virginia', deadly, venomous snakes are ritually caressed and handled at regular religious ceremonies. Slithering piles of rattlesnakes are dumped on the floor of the church, grasped in bare hands and lifted high. They are challenged to do their handlers harm. As the congregation sings and sways and claps its hands, the main performers coil the lethal snakes around their bodies. The snakes – including the deadliest of all North American snakes, the five-foot-long Eastern Diamondback Rattlesnake – are completely untreated. Their venom fangs are intact and fully operative, a fact readily proved by the occasional accident when a handler is bitten. There are, of course, local laws against the handling of dangerous animals, as there are today in most Western countries, but in the case of these Christian fanatics they are, diplomatically, never enforced. Their enforcement would amount to religious suppression, so a blind eye is turned.

These fundamentalist snake-handlers are outraged at the suggestion that they are engaging in serpent-worship. They see the snakes as living embodiments of the Devil and the object of their rituals is to test the strength of their Christian faith: if it is strong enough, it will beat the Devil and they will remain unscathed. Amazingly most of them are not harmed, although occasionally the faith is not quite strong enough, or perhaps the grip on the snakes is a little too strong, and the irritated animals lash out and inject their venom into the handlers' flesh. The results are not pleasant to watch, as the human tissues become swollen, distorted and discoloured. The pain is excruciating, but bitten handlers are soon back at their devotions, once again covered in writhing snakes. Deaths are rare, but they do occur. Indeed, by a sad irony, the founder of the movement, a circuit preacher, died of snakebite in 1955.

Objective investigators have puzzled over the small number of bites that occur, bearing in mind that each church has several snake-handling meetings every week. The only unusual observation concerning the handlers is that they appear to enter a trancelike condition in which their extremities are exceptionally cold. It is thought that this could reduce the reaction of the snakes to being grasped, and it has uncharitably been suggested that the snakes themselves are mildly refrigerated before being handled. This would have the effect of rendering them torpid and slow to respond, but there seems to be little evidence that this is the case. The truth is that, if handled casually, most snakes – even the most venomous ones – are reluctant to strike. Every strike wastes precious venom which is desperately needed for prey-killing and survival. The extraordinary snake-handlers of the United States may have discovered that, even in the hand, the snake is not as dangerous as popular legend would suggest. However, a true believer will prefer the conclusion that the handlers are demonstrating that Christian faith is stronger than the Devil in the serpent's body.

The American snake-handling cult dates only from 1909, but it reflects an attitude that is centuries old. Egypt was not alone in worshipping snakes, and serpent cults arose in many other places, including ancient Greece. As time has passed, the original intensity of these cults' rituals has been dissipated: the snake, once the object of an ancient form of worship, has become instead an object of entertainment.

Lying beneath the American snake-handlers' religious beliefs there is probably a deeper, unconscious level of human experience where risk-taking has its own peculiar reward. This is rooted in the days when to challenge a dangerous animal and win was part and parcel of everyday human existence. The excitement of the challenge is exploited wherever unfortunate serpents are used for the amusement of tourists. Tormented and manhandled, these snakes arouse little pity. The magnificent python, for example, set free in a circle of spectators only to be recaptured by its handlers in a gratuitous display of courage, is seen not as the remarkable end-point of an extraordinary evolutionary story, but as a dangerous animal to be subdued and publicly degraded. In such spectacles, the performers play on man's deep-seated fear of snakes. Given the mythology of evil that has also grown up around the snake, it is not surprising that the audience is alarmed and impressed by the crudely melodramatic act of domination taking place in front of them.

The snakecharmer's cobra is another victim of this ancient

fear. In fact its lips are sealed, so that it is entirely harmless, and it is then endlessly aggravated to earn money for its owner. The snakecharmer pretends to entrance his serpent with sacred music but the ritual is a phoney one, since all snakes are totally deaf. This ridiculous sideshow highlights the degree to which we can misunderstand the true nature of our animal companions if we approach them as symbols instead of as complex living beings: as symbols they have no feelings and are vulnerable to any of our human whims and fancies.

This lack of respect for other animals was accentuated by a shift in religious attitudes. Under the growing influence of the early Christian Church, all forms of animal worship had come under attack. Everywhere the snake cults were suppressed as representing the epitome of pagan depravity.

By the seventeenth century a famous naturalist, otherwise intent on a calm, scientific presentation of animal life, could not resist the temptation to write: 'Ever since the Devil entered into the serpent it became hateful to all. Serpents are the most ungentle and barbarous of creatures.' Another naturalist, writing in the eighteenth century, stressed the need to be vigilant in case the serpent became once again a revered, holy creature: 'The Devil, who under the shape of the serpent, tempted our first parents, has with unwearied application laboured to deify that animal, as a trophy of his first victory over mankind.' Such was the hatred towards snakes whipped up by the Church that there was little fear of any pro-serpent lobby gaining a religious upper hand again. The only exception to this was a curious group of Gnostics called Ophites who believed that the Virgin Mary had experienced an unusual encounter with a serpent, resulting in Christ as a reincarnation of that serpent. The worship of Christ as the serpent never caught on, however, and faded away in the very early days of the Christian epoch. With it faded respect, not only for snakes, but for all non-human animals. A new era in relations between man and other animals was dawning.

*　　*　　*

It is clear that, in the earliest phase of the Animal Contract, primitive reverence for other creatures was a mixed blessing. From prehistoric hunters to sophisticated Egyptian urbanites, there was huge respect for certain animals, but largely as totems, symbols, emblems or sacred beings. If they stood for something good, they were treated well. If they stood for something bad, they were persecuted. The division was an arbitrary one, dependent on the whims of superstitious priests and holy men, whose thoughts were focused more on power on earth and glory in heaven than on the well-being of their fellow creatures.

However, even that part of the ancient social contract in which humans respected other creatures as their spiritual kin was to be broken down by a new concept that placed mankind above all other species. Now only man was deemed to have a soul. Other animals were reduced to 'brute beasts of no understanding'. For Christians, with God at the head of this new social order, humans in the middle, and animals at the bottom, the scene was set for mindless persecution of all other species. Since animals were seen as soulless brutes, there was no guilt involved in killing them. Indeed, the holy writings contained instructions about how man should behave towards other animals: the new, almighty God ordered him to multiply and subdue the earth, holding dominion over all other creatures. If man shared the company of animals, it was not to honour them as spiritual kin or to worship them as divine manifestations. They could be laughed at as caricatures of ourselves put there to remind us of our superiority, over-powered in displays of spurious courage, enslaved as humble beasts of burden, or tormented for entertainment. The period of Christian domination cannot be described as a good one for animals.

It is curious that a religion professing gentleness and kindness should have been the cause of so much animal suffer-ing. How did this come about?

One of the great weaknesses of the Bible is that, between its covers, it is possible to find a quotation to justify almost any attitude. By careful selection it is a simple matter to draw completely opposing conclusions concerning correct human conduct. In order to depict the human condition as vastly superior to that of other creatures, it is only necessary to quote Genesis, where God tells Noah that 'the fear of you and the dread of you shall be upon every beast of the earth . . . into your hands are they delivered'. By giving mankind dominion over all other forms of life, God apparently makes it clear that we can do more or less as we wish with animals and clearly have no close kinship with them.

From this starting point there developed a trend in Christian thought that led to appalling cruelties in later cen-turies. It took some time to gather strength and, to be fair to the Christian Church, the earliest attitudes were far more friendly towards our animal companions. Indeed, at first, there was no antagonism towards the idea that humans and other animals are closely related. Had he lived in the fourth century, Darwin would have been delighted to hear a Christian saint proclaiming that we should be kind to animals because 'they are of the same origin as ourselves'. This enlightened view stemmed from other statements in the Bible that stress our affinity with animals. However, despite the work of people such as St Francis, this attitude eventually died away, overpowered by the need to sustain man's dominant role in the world. This was partly due to the need to justify slavery. If it was acceptable to treat certain types of human being as inferiors with no rights, then how could rights be given to mammals, birds, reptiles or fish? To the medieval mind the idea was nonsensical.

Under the influence of the thirteenth-century writings of Thomas Aquinas and with the advent of the Inquisition, the Christian Church embarked upon centuries of sanctified torment, torture and murder. Nearly a million people were put to death for failing to conform to the narrow rules of the pious. Many of them were said to be witches, whose crimes could include consorting with animals thought to be in league with the Devil. Any religious activity or superstitious practice that involved association with animals of any kind was considered the height of wickedness. Heretics who claimed that animals had souls, like humans, were savagely persecuted. Thousands were massacred in Europe for this belief. All animal cults were suppressed and eliminated with great severity. The human species was being purged of any significant connection with other species of animals.

The only relations possible in such times were purely economic ones. Farm animals were treated brutally but remained important sources of food. Beasts of burden were worked until they dropped. Many wild beasts were tortured for entertainment, as were bulls and other impressive domestic stock. Bull-baiting was defended as a sport that tested courage and improved the mind. The Church approved and encouraged this attitude because it helped to keep mankind at the pinnacle of creation, superior to all other forms of life.

Reforms did not gain ground until as recently as the nineteenth century, when animal welfare organisations began to establish themselves and sow the seeds of a new relationship with animal life. The priesthood was now split. Some demanded a return to kindness to all living things, while others persisted in the old approach of maintaining man's superiority. The Catholic Church was strongly opposed to the new enlightenment and Pope Pius IX, to his shame, even refused permission for the opening of an animal welfare centre in Rome. The reason he gave was that, in giving time and thought to animals, attention would be taken away from human considerations.

At the end of the nineteenth century, the *Catholic Dictionary* was able to state categorically that animals 'have no rights. The brutes are made for man who has the same right over them which he has over plants and stones.' Astonishingly, the statement continues with the ultimate in callousness, declaring that it is 'lawful to put them to death, or to inflict pain upon them, for any good or reasonable end . . . even for the purpose of recreation'.

The date of this statement is 1897. Nearly a century later its echoes can still be heard, despite the fact that we have witnessed a massive revolution against such an unfeeling philosophy. The old ideas cling to our language: we still use animal terms as insults; we still hound animals to death for pleasure; we still torture bulls to death in front of paying customers. The Christian legacy remains. We still feel ourselves to be superior beings with a licence to use the rest of the world as we wish. Far too many of us still subscribe, albeit rather quietly, to the dictum of the Jesuit priest who, at the turn of the century, said, 'Brute beasts, not having under-standing and therefore not being persons, cannot have any rights . . . We have no duties of charity, nor duties of any kind, to the lower animals.'

Those of us who have entirely abandoned this position often forget how deeply ingrained the old attitudes are in our civilised world. In the post-Darwinian epoch, when it is clear to any intelligent being that man and the other animals are close relatives, it is sometimes hard to accept that the medieval witch-hunters are still lurking in the shadows of our cities and stalking our countryside. They are there and they resurface at the slightest excuse. Until the Christian Church totally and officially repudiates its earlier attitude towards animals, the danger will always be there.

*　　*　　*

One of the lasting consequences of the attitude that man is superior to animals is what could be called the Cartooning of Animals. To make them safe we make them into amusing caricatures, as if they were ridiculous imposters worthy only of our derisive laughter. The reason for this is not hard to find. Nearly all animals have features that are reminiscent of human beings: they have a pair of eyes, a mouth, a nose; they play and jump and run; they grow from babies into adults; and they show many behaviour patterns that parallel human activities. It is hardly surprising that we can see ourselves reflected in them. For those who believe in evolution this can be accepted as natural kinship. For others who believe in the great divide between us and them, their similarities to us are an embarrassment. They make us feel uncomfortable. One solution is to see the similarities as foolish imitations, and the animals as clowns sent to amuse us.

For centuries there have been animal entertainments: at fairs, in the streets, in theatres and in the circus ring. From the organ-grinder's monkey to the dancing bear, they have given us that satisfying glow of superiority as we witness their antics. The fact that each one of these animal entertainers is greatly superior to the human species in certain aspects is carefully overlooked. We choose the terms on which they are to perform and they are always our terms, so our position is not challenged.

If, by chance, they possess a feature that is inescapably superior to ours, then we have to apply a new rule. This states that if an animal is particularly good at something, we must devise an entertainment that belittles this quality. The most obvious example is brute strength. The lion, the tiger and the elephant are clearly much stronger than we are, so we arrange spectacles in which they are dominated by human skill and cunning. The lion-tamer cracks his whip and the lion jumps through a hoop; the elephant-trainer raises his stick and the mighty beast bows before us. The lion has been made a craven coward for our amusement, the elephant a lumbering idiot. We cheer and clap our hands at this crude enactment of human power over nature.

Of all the creatures exploited in this way, none has been so elaborately employed as the monkey. As our closest relatives, monkeys and apes are endowed with qualities that make them ideal material for caricaturing human beings. They have suffered this undignified fate for centuries. Even in ancient times, according to the Roman poet Juvenal, monkeys were dressed up and expected to perform for our amusement. One famous monkey, entertaining the public near the city wall, was trained to ride a goat and hurl a javelin, while wearing a helmet and carrying a shield.

During the Middle Ages travelling showmen frequently included a performing monkey – usually a Barbary ape from North Africa – in their displays. These medieval monkeys are reputed to have played musical instruments, and early manuscripts show them doing just this. It is doubtful whether they managed to pick out a tune, but simply to strike the instruments and create some kind of sound would have been enough to demonstrate both that they wanted to imitate humans and that they failed miserably in the attempt. When jousting on horseback was popular, monkeys were trained to burlesque the noble knights. They were forced to perform their own mock-jousts, mounted on the backs of large dogs. Even today, mounted monkeys can still be seen in the more primitive travelling circuses.

Performing monkeys were popular all over the world. In Japan stump-tailed macaques were employed as assistants by jugglers. In Egypt baboons were employed as clowns. In South America capuchin monkeys were so adept at their comic performances that many were imported to Europe, where they eventually became the traditional organ-grinder's monkey. The capuchins proved to be the most intelligent actors of all, some being trained to beg for silver coins. The subtlety of their routine astonished the onlookers. One, for example, would hold out its hand for a coin and then, if given a silver one, would doff its hat to the donor. If it was a nickel coin, the monkey would merely touch its hat and give a discreet cough. If the coin was valueless, the animal would hold it up for close inspection and then ostentatiously throw it away. If nothing was given, it would stand and scream at the miser in question. The capuchin carried a purse with separate compartments for the different coins and always placed the correct coin in the correct compartment. Such refinements never ceased to amaze the onlookers, but even in their admiration they still regarded the monkeys as no more than amusing clowns.

It was this element of admiration that perpetuated animal entertainments long after people had become genuinely sensitive to the exploitation that was taking place. Even in the present century, parents have taken their offspring to see the performing animals in the circus ring, not because they are as cruel and thoughtless as their predecessors, but because of the joy and excitement that shone on the children's faces. Privately they may have been concerned about how the circus trainers managed to make the wild beasts stand on their heads or jump through flaming hoops, but the intense pleasure they saw on the young faces around them more than compensated for their misgivings. As a result, the circus managed to survive with its animal acts intact long after a more enlightened view of animals had grown strong in society. The circus became an anomaly, a medieval survival that refused to die out.

The reaction of modern children to circus animals is easy to understand. Encountering a monkey, a lion or an elephant at close quarters for the first time is an astonishing experience. The novelty of the beasts is breathtaking if you have never been so close to one before. The sheer wonder of the animal forms provides such a dazzling spectacle that all other considerations are swept aside. The children cannot be blamed for this response. Their childhood has been full of images of cuddly toy animals, of animals in fairy-tales and Disney cartoons. The first real animals they see in the flesh are merely extensions of the toy ones and are treated as such. However, the failure to make the distinction between animals and toys involves us in a distortion of the animals so that they are seen as humble brutes, performing tricks and stunts to fulfil their part in an Animal Contract that states: you make us laugh and we will feed you.

Today the circus is under attack and in many areas animal acts are forbidden. Opponents of the circus claim that the animals are cruelly treated and that circus training always involves severe punishments. This is unfair to circus people, most of whom are devoted to their animals. Cruelty is a poor tool where dangerous animals are concerned; much more common is great patience and kindness.

This does not excuse what happens in the circus ring. Even if it can be proved that circus animals enjoy an exciting and varied life, with more benefits than disadvantages, the circus performance remains a demeaning spectacle. If, as children, we adored these furry clowns as living animal toys, we meant them no harm. Yet in our friendly fun we utterly degraded them. The true criticism against circuses should be that they show animals in a distorting mirror that has warped our understanding of them. It is for this reason that animal acts are fading into history.

*   *   *

The history of zoos has not been a happy one for animals. Early zoos were little more than freak shows; some even included human freaks in their cages alongside the wild beasts. The largest known zoo was discovered by Spanish explorers when they first came across the ancient American empire of the Aztecs. The Aztec ruler, Montezuma, was an animal fanatic and his magnificent collection of birds and beasts of prey was tended by no fewer than 600 keepers – the largest zoo staff ever known. Five hundred turkeys were killed every day to feed his birds of prey alone, and it was rumoured that his larger cats (pumas and jaguars) dined regularly on human flesh. An eye-witness reported, 'These beasts and the frightful reptiles are held there to keep their hellish gods company, and when these animals roar and hiss the palace seems like hell itself.' The atmosphere could not have been improved by the fact that the emperor 'kept men and women monsters, some crippled, others dwarfed or hunchbacked' in his zoo, along with a collection of human albinos.

Other great leaders also devoted much energy to animal collections. Three thousand years ago, in the Far East, the Chinese rulers developed zoos which Kublai Khan, the Great Khan, expanded when he came to power. For him they were not a way of satisfying curiosity about animal life, or of displaying high status, but were primarily an adjunct to hunting. The beasts and birds of prey he kept were allowed to chase and kill the other inmates of his zoo parks: the zoo was a convenient arena for easy hunting.

In Europe, captive animals did not fare much better in ancient times. The Roman menageries were also secondary to the main business: the mass slaughter of animals in the great amphitheatres.

As the centuries passed a less bloodthirsty attitude developed. When the great explorers set sail to discover new lands around the globe they marvelled at the exotic creatures they found, many of which were brought back to be displayed to their countrymen. Royal figures became fascinated and established their own personal aviaries or menageries. The inmates rarely lived for very long after their exhausting journeys, since little was known about the special needs of the exotic species. They were ill-fed, ill-housed, and soon became diseased and died, but their appeal persisted. More and more were brought back to satisfy regal curiosity. No thought was given to the plight of the animals concerned. They were still regarded as 'brute beasts', and only their rarity and costliness gave them protection from human indifference. Where the public was admitted, visitors were sometimes given the opportunity to buy long sticks with which to prod the captive animals, to make them move and react in a more amusing manner. Few of the cages or enclosures gave their occupants even a hint of their natural habitat, and little attempt was made to establish breeding groups.

In the early nineteenth century the zoological collection of the newly formed Zoological Society of London was established. It was this collection that was to give the name 'zoo' to the world, but its foundation was not motivated by the simple scientific desire to study wild animals. There was a much more practical reason: the increased exploitation of wildlife by human beings. The founders of the zoo pointed out that all the species of domestic animals then in use had been bred long ago. It seemed extraordinary that an advanced culture could not improve on them. The zoo founders commented that, since all previous domestication was due 'to the efforts of savage or uncultivated nations, it is impossible not to hope for many new, brilliant and useful results in the same field, by the application of the wealth, ingenuity, and varied resources of a civilised people'. For this reason, the principal aim of the Zoological Society of London was to be the 'introducing and domesticating of new Breeds or Varieties of Animals . . . likely to be useful in Common Life'.

In this respect the society has been a miserable failure. Apart from releasing the grey squirrel on an unsuspecting British countryside, the only new introduction for which the learned society appears to have been responsible is that of the golden hamster, which has become a favourite domestic pet of millions of children. This is not what the founders of the society had in mind. They visualised the zoo as a hotbed for the production of new domestic animals which would revolutionise agriculture and animal husbandry. Today, nearly two centuries later, we still farm with almost precisely the same animal breeds that we employed before the zoo was formed.

Instead of pursuing its original aims, the zoo in London became a major scientific institution, building up the greatest collection of wild species ever seen. It did this on a small plot of land — less than 40 acres — in the middle of London. Cramped, crowded, and wholly unsuitable for such a grand plan, the gardens of the Zoological Society were filled with Victorian cages, heavy with bars and thick with wires. The public was permitted to feed the inmates and to come into close proximity with them. The small, bare enclosures were scrubbed clean in the manner of a human prison or poor-house. The captives, bored, frustrated and deprived of almost all natural activities, quickly became animal lunatics in a noisy asylum: victims of the naked cage.

Anyone studying these wretched creatures could observe that their behaviour had become hopelessly abnormal. Many became pathological overeaters, growing immensely fat and unhealthy. One bear literally ate itself to death, dying of suffocation from the pressure of fat and gobbled food. Others became pathological pacers, walking neurotically up and down in a bizarre, stereotyped pattern of movement that eventually wore a track in the surface of their enclosures. Still others became dung-eaters, self-mutilators, or self-starvers. Aberrant sexual behaviour became commonplace, some isolated animals even attempting to copulate with their food bowls, or with other totally inappropriate species with which they were housed. There is something grotesque about a squirrel trying to bury a nut, a wild dog trying to dig a hole for a bone, or a wildcat trying to cover its faeces, when they are all scratching at concrete floors. The lessons such menageries teach us are little better than the message we get from the circus: wild animals are to be caught and subdued for our pleasure.

Despite increasing knowledge concerning the true environmental needs of captive animals, the zoos of the world were slow to reform. By the middle of the twentieth century little had been done. One can only wonder why we have for so long taken pleasure in abusing animals in this way. Religious dogma may originally have licensed us to act in this manner, but why have we been so keen to renew that licence year after year, even when our religious passion has waned so extensively? Given that the animals were so bored and miserable, why were the early zoos so popular? The answer lies in the terrible isolation from wildlife that resulted from the blossoming of huge cities, especially after the industrial revolution.

Before the advent of cinema and television, city-dwellers rarely encountered wild animals in any form. For them, a visit to the city zoo must have been a major excitement. The animals they saw there acted as unhappy ambassadors for their species, reminding this alienated population that wonderful creatures existed somewhere in the world. Even after the arrival of the cinema screen in the cities, the animals seen there were not shown in their true light. They were usually depicted as savage beasts, attacking our hero or being gunned down by brave hunters. Sometimes they were naughty chimps making us giggle. True-life nature films were yet to come.

When television further expanded the world of the trapped urbanite, the small black-and-white picture failed to do the animal world justice. There were more documentaries but they still could not fire the imagination.

Following the invention of colour television in the late 1960s, many magnificent natural history films were made and shown across the world. A whole generation grew up with an awareness of what wild animals were really like in their natural homes. At the same time, the study of ethology – the scientific discipline that brings a naturalistic approach to the analysis of animal behaviour – was making great strides. Working together, ethologists and film-makers produced more and more penetrating studies of the lives of wild animals. These left no doubt as to the shortcomings of the earlier ways of seeing these fascinating creatures.

It is no coincidence that, since the end of the 1960s, the fortunes of the world's zoos have been steadily declining. In a recent survey, 81 per cent of the respondents voted against keeping animals in zoos. London Zoo is no longer packed with happy families. It is in grave financial difficulties, and for the first time in its long history has had to seek outside assistance. The final nails in its Victorian coffin were the magnificent television series *Life on Earth* and *The Living Planet*. Taking six years to make, involving huge numbers of specialist photographers and literally millions of miles of travel around the globe, these 'windows on the wild' brought the true splendour of animal life into everyone's living room. After people had seen the grace and beauty of lions on the African plains, they would find it hard to accept the bored inmates of a zoo cage as being worthy of their attention.

The traditional zoo was dead but not buried. Its cages were built to last. Only a massive, active antagonism could bring in the bulldozers. Although enthusiasm had been replaced by apathy, there was not enough hostility to sweep them away. Small anti-zoo groups did emerge and demand reforms. They attacked zoos as 'animal concentration camps' where, all too often, the animals were the objects of laughter and derision. They depicted captivity as inevitably, inherently cruel and all zoo visitors as insensitive, crass and stupid. They wanted to see a complete end to zoos throughout the world.

These attacks were unfair. Despite their obvious limitations, the early zoos did, in their time, play a major role in reminding the urban world of the wild wonders beyond the suburbs. For many zoo visitors they were the only lifeline to nature, a slender thread that helped to encourage an interest in living things. The zoo authorities had done their best to bring an element of education into their activities, but their end-of-term report read 'means well, must try harder'.

Increasingly conscious of their limitations, modern zoos have struggled manfully to rid themselves of their Victorian image and to provide their inmates with better conditions wherever possible. This has led to some highly ingenious and scientifically rewarding exhibits. In the best establishments, new technology has been installed to provide near-ideal conditions for even the most demanding species. Our knowledge of the social behaviour of many kinds of animals means that they can be kept in natural breeding groups in their much more complex enclosures. The successful breeding that results means in turn that today's zoos no longer need to plunder the wild populations for further stock. They can produce their own and exchange specimens with other zoos, via an international network of co-operation.

These improvements make it possible for the new-style, more sensitive visitor to enjoy a visit to one of the best of modern zoos and to learn a great deal in the process. The direct impact of the living animal still works its magic in a way that electronic images or photographs can never do. Good modern zoos clearly retain an important role in fostering our relations with other animals.

Some of the greatest advances are, inevitably, being made by the biggest zoos, such as the one at San Diego, but some of the smaller zoos are also making pioneering changes. The new tropical enclosure at Arnhem Zoo in Holland, for example, is about as far away as it is possible to get from the old-fashioned Victorian zoo cage. A vast, covered area kept at tropical heat and humidity all the year round, it has been heavily planted with tropical vegetation. Complete with natural streams and even waterfalls, it is a feast for the eyes. The paths that criss-cross it allow the visitor to wander around freely in a jungle setting, exploring for animals as if momentarily in another land. There are 1500 animals somewhere inside the enclosure, but they are not at first obvious: the visitor has to search for them. There are reptiles basking on the river-banks, small birds flitting through the bushes, fish darting through the water, exotic butterflies fluttering from plant to plant. There is nothing large to be seen and nothing is thrust at the onlooker. This is an entirely new style of zoo exhibit in which the visitor must work for his discoveries. It gives a taste of what it is like to be out in the wilds on a genuine field trip. This type of enclosure could herald a whole new chapter in zoo display. It is light years away from the old idea of a small, hygienic, naked cage: instead it is a place that celebrates the zoo inmate.

One of the major strengths of these smaller zoos is that they can specialise in certain types of animal. The specialist zoos probably offer one of the best hopes for the future because they can concentrate their efforts and become experts on a small segment of the wild fauna, rather than dabbling simultaneously in many areas. This is reflected in a second brave venture at Arnhem, where a remarkable chimpanzee colony has been established. It epitomises the new approach to the keeping of animals in zoos and embodies three important principles.

Firstly, it makes use of all our recent scientific discoveries concerning the behaviour of chimpanzees in the wild to give these animals the most appropriate social setting and environment. The zoo has constructed a large island enclosure of a kind that provides a living space sufficiently rich and varied to satisfy these most intelligent of apes. The social composition of the initial chimpanzee population was calculated so as to provide the ideal group for later breeding. As a result, these animals live a complex social life, never become bored, and have already bred to the third generation. Over 100 baby chimps have been born, and with the wild homes of this species so much at risk, the colony has become a little oasis of chimpanzees, safe and secure for the future.

Secondly, it provides a study centre for students of animal behaviour, where more can be learned about these, our closest animal relatives. Our understanding of chimpanzee social life and intelligence has already been greatly advanced by the observations made at Arnhem Zoo. High above the island enclosure there is a research observation post equipped with video cameras and other recording devices. These monitor even the tiniest details of ape behaviour that could not be detected easily in the wild, where so much is hidden from human eyes. University students work there throughout the year, amassing information that has already made us rethink some of our ideas about these extraordinary animals.

Thirdly, it gives the public an unhindered view of the chimpanzees by banishing wire-mesh and heavy iron bars and replacing them with a simple water-ditch. Since apes cannot swim, this ditch is all that is necessary to retain them and offers the public a much greater sense of intimacy with the animals they are watching. In short, it is a zoo exhibit where everyone benefits.

Sadly, however, there remain many smaller zoos of the old-fashioned kind, with bleak, naked cages and neurotically bored and frustrated inmates. A recent survey of European zoos revealed that, although there were only 218 registered in the *International Zoo Yearbook*, there were in reality 1007 in the countries of the European Community alone. Of the nearly 800 unregistered zoos, many 'displayed sheer ignorance. Ignorance of the animals' basic needs, ignorance of design and ignorance of the amount of money needed to keep them.' Some of the animals were, to quote the investigator, 'the most lifeless or psychotic I have ever witnessed'. Clearly zoos have a long way to go and the bad ones can so easily tarnish the reputations of all zoos, including the genuinely improved ones.

The development of the more enlightened animal displays reflects an increasing concern about what we have been doing to wild animals in the past. Our new awareness is driving us towards a more naturalistic style of zoo-keeping, but this creates an uncomfortable contradiction: we must devise captivity that does not look like captivity, and pretend that these are wild animals in the wild, even though we know that they are not.

Safari parks have followed this approach. Here whole herds of game and troops of monkeys can move about freely, while it is the human observers who are restricted to metal and glass cages. The animals have the freedom to move, while the humans are restricted. It is essentially a good Animal Contract, although there are two snags: exhaust fumes and the problem of winter quarters. The safari parks at stately homes in Europe have become immensely popular and they do answer many of the criticisms levelled at the traditional city zoos, but if their popularity continues to increase it will certainly become necessary to install small electric cars to replace the larger petrol vehicles and reduce the chemical pollution. Otherwise, the animals will be suffering from life in a permanent traffic jam. There is also the problem of keeping tropical animals in a northern climate. Visitors usually only flock to the safari parks in the summer months. They do not see the tropical animals suffering during the long, cold winters. Until much more elaborate, heated winter quarters are provided, the safari parks must be viewed with only limited approval. They are an exciting new departure, but they still need to be perfected. The parks would benefit from becoming more specialised, for example, with each park becoming really expert at keeping just a few kinds of animals, rather than attempting to provide an apology for a Noah's Ark.

Some zoos have introduced a variation on the concept of the caged human: the animals are free to clamber around in the treetops, but the humans must walk through a long wire tunnel in order to study them. The protective wire is a nuisance, but it only interferes with the human visitors, not the zoo animals. This is the method adopted at Monkey Jungle in Florida, where the primates live out a near-natural life in the branches, while the visitors are relegated to the role of 'inmates'. Smaller monkeys which are neither too shy nor too aggressive can be seen in spacious walk-through enclosures.

Monkeys such as marmosets scamper busily about in the heavily planted undergrowth as their human observers move slowly through their leafy world. This is a method that has often been used with birds in the past but far too rarely with other animals, many of which quickly adapt to this lifestyle and flourish in it.

To the purists, however, all zoos and captive animal displays are unacceptable. To them, the very act of placing an animal in captivity is invalid: an exploitation rather than a celebration of the species in question. They wish to see all wild animals left in the wild, free from human intervention. They argue that we can now all enjoy watching these animals living in nature and behaving naturally, either by visiting them in the wild, or by seeing them in films and on television, so that the excuses for keeping them in captivity have gone. Even if we cannot observe certain of the wild animals, it is enough simply to know that they are there, living out their lives and sharing the planet with us. We should leave them in peace. Zoos may be caring for animals for their own sake and honouring this type of contract to the utmost of their ability, but is this more than the Southern gentlemen being exceptionally kind to their slaves? Did that justify slavery? Does this justify captive animals?

If zoos are eventually banned it will be a tragedy, because they have so much to teach us, not only as visitors but also as professional students of wildlife. In an ideal world, every child should have the opportunity to visit wild places and see wild animals in their natural habitat. This is clearly not possible. In an ideal world every wild animal should be allowed to live untouched by human interference in its native territories, but this is increasingly unlikely as the human population swells by another 150,000 people a day, every day. If our new-found sensibilities make us feel that there is something wrong with the zoo concept, then the answer is to stop overpopulating the world.

With wild habitats disappearing at an alarming rate, the day will come when zoos are the only wildlife survival zones we have. Even the great game parks of the tropics will have shrunk to little more than glorified zoo parks. We will need all the knowledge we can muster to assist us in keeping the remnants of the wild fauna alive and well. That is where the good, modern zoos will come into their own, for they are accumulating more and more expertise in the delicate matter of wildlife management. We simply cannot risk losing this expertise.

*　　*　　*

The position in the oceans might seem to be different: so far they have defied human settlement and their vast territories appear to be comparatively safe. However, they are already polluted and even their future may be in doubt.

For years the traditional aquarium with its rows of glass tanks has provided a glimpse of the dazzling variety of life to be found in the underwater world. The environment provided for the fish and other creatures has been less offensive than the naked cages of the birds and mammals in zoos, but appearances are deceptive. The fact is that the majority of aquarium inmates fail to breed and have to be replaced even more often than zoo inmates. This has applied especially to marine life.

Attempts to improve conditions in the public aquarium have lagged behind those in the zoo. With the exception of marine mammals, aquatic animals generally fail to arouse strong protective emotions, so there has been little pressure on aquarium staff to modernise their exhibits. This is clearly reflected in the widespread acceptance of the sport of angling. If millions of people went into the countryside each week to hook small mammals and birds with a rod and line there would be an outcry against such a cruel practice, but few voices are raised against the hooking of fish from rivers and lakes for the fun of seeing who can catch the biggest one. The suggestion that it hurts the fish less is based on ignorance. Aquatic animals suffer from the disadvantage that they cannot scream when in pain, so we find it hard to gauge the degree of their agony. If fish could scream, angling purely for sport would be outlawed without delay.

Against this background it is easy to see how the public aquarium has failed to advance, despite growing knowledge from a wide variety of aquatic behaviour studies. We have the information necessary to improve captive conditions: all we need is the impetus to implement them. In a few instances this has been achieved with dramatic results. In Australia and North America there have been several impressive new aquarium developments, where huge installations have made it possible for visitors to watch virtually natural marine environments. As at Monkey Jungle, the humans are restricted but the other species are not. Underwater glass tunnels take the viewers through the sub-aquatic world and reveal what the old-fashioned aquaria have been lacking for so long: the miraculous elegance of marine life. These spectacular innovations must surely herald a new approach, for once seen they will create a new demand for much higher standards.

This is a new kind of zoo altogether, with the minimum of intrusion and the maximum of freedom for the animals. Even the purists would find this kind of exhibit hard to fault. It promotes intimacy with wildlife without exploitation.

In the meantime, marine mammals have experienced mixed fortunes peculiar to their own kind. Whales, for example, have suffered years of uncontrolled slaughter, but new knowledge of the world of cetaceans has led to some rethinking. First came the discovery that these huge animals were being brought to the verge of extinction. Then came the revelation that, far from being vast, insensitive mountains of blubber, they were extremely complex beings with an elaborate communication system and a level of mental development that aroused a wholly new outpouring of human sympathy. Underwater films of whales and recordings of their amazing song routines transformed them into star personalities. The idea of firing harpoons into them now seemed the height of barbarity. When three whales were trapped in ice in 1988, public interest in their plight reached such a pitch that North American and Russian resources were combined to the tune of $1 million to rescue them and release them into the open seas. Captain Ahab would never have believed it.

It is hard to understand how any human being could ever have taken pleasure in the butchery of such extraordinary creatures. The sheer scale of the slaughter – the gallons of blood, the towering piles of flesh – seems utterly nauseating. Yet early whalers revelled in it. The leading whalers were all devout Christians – usually fundamentalists – and they looked upon the whale as the most hideous incarnation of the forces of evil, describing it as 'the great gliding demon of the seas of life'. It seems that the whale's lack of legs somehow caused it to be confused with the much-hated snake and converted it into the giant serpent-to-end-all-serpents. Its open mouth was sometimes depicted as the gateway to hell and the Book of Job reinforced the Christian approach to the way the monster should be treated, asking, 'Canst thou draw out leviathan with an hook? or his tongue with a cord which thou lettest down? Canst thou put an hook into his nose? or bore his jaw through with a thorn? . . . Canst thou fill his skin with barbed irons? or his head with fish spears?' For the captains of the early whaling ships the Bible was tantamount to a hunting manual, giving helpful hints in addition to moral justification for the carnage.

The smaller relatives of the whales, the dolphins and porpoises, escaped the giant's evil reputation and, indeed, gained some degree of protection from superstitious beliefs. Because they were reported to be friendly to men, especially sailors, it was considered unlucky to harm them. Their playfulness intrigued the ancients and their helpfulness became woven into classical legends.

It is these characteristics that have made them such attractive subjects for captive displays. They have been kept in captivity since the fifteenth century, but it was not until the twentieth century that their popularity demanded what amounted to a new kind of zoo especially for them: the marineland. When they were first exhibited in these specially designed marine pools it is reported that they soon became restless. Their naturally high level of playfulness demanded some kind of outlet for which their hygienic new enclosures made no provision. All they could find were some pebbles on the floor of the giant tank. These they picked up in their mouths and threw at the visitors. They singled out nuns in particular for their attacks: it seems that the holy sisters' black habits reminded the dolphins of some traditional marine enemy, perhaps sea-lions. The marineland owners, horrified by these attacks on paying customers, quickly removed all pebbles from the dolphin pool, which now became boringly sterile. The reaction of the dolphins was to sink into a deep depression.

Equally alarmed by this reaction, the owners tried to find other ways of keeping the animals occupied. They threw a ball into the pool and were delighted to observe that the animals soon started playing with it, pushing it around with their noses. More and more playthings were added to the pool and soon the animals were busily keeping themselves amused. The visitors were fascinated and it was only a short step from this random play to a carefully structured public performance. Tiered seating was added and regular shows put on for the growing audience. The dolphins learnt to leap through hoops, jump in unison, play basketball, catch rings on their noses, pull small boats around the pool with children in them, and even leap out of the water to be kissed by their trainers. The animals' depression was banished and the crowds were delighted. A new type of animal enthralment had been born. Marinelands quickly appeared all over the world and, in the second half of the twentieth century, they have become a major commercial venture.

The marineland is an extremely popular entertainment. It is impossible not to marvel at the dolphins' performances, and yet there is something wrong. The problem is that we are once again in the circus ring. In the marineland there is no attempt to subdue and dominate the animals, and no cruelty is involved in their training because there is no need for it. Indeed, it would be cruel not to train them, once captive. The crowds react with awe and wonder at the beauty and skill of the dolphins as much as they laugh at their antics. In the end, however, the performance is artificial and contrived, reducing these amazing creatures to the level of hired entertainers. To the audience they remain caricatures, performing animal tricks reminiscent of the medieval dancing bears and monkeys. It is a regression to a more primitive attitude.

The dolphinariums and marinelands neatly sum up the dilemma of the modern zoo world. Keeping animals in captivity automatically involves artificiality. If that artificiality is an empty cage, the animal goes mad with boredom. If it is the zoo equivalent of a circus ring, the public views the animal through a distorting mirror. If attempts are made to create what looks like a miniature version of the natural habitat of the animal, it can hardly ever be as complex as the real thing: it may look better than the old-style cages, but it remains essentially inferior to the wild environment.

As far as dolphins are concerned, there is really no excuse for keeping them in captivity. They are naturally friendly and co-operative creatures, who regularly swim near the shore to enjoy the company of humans. There are fully authenticated cases of dolphins and fishermen working together to catch fish. In the Mediterranean, for example, recent studies have revealed a remarkable case of mutual aid in trapping mullet. When the local fishermen detect a large shoal of the fish swimming near the shore, they beat the water with sticks. This attracts the local dolphins to the scene. The fishermen cast their nets and the shoal is hemmed in between the fishermen on one side and the dolphins on the other. In their panic the fish are easy for both men and dolphins to catch. The most surprising feature of this co-operative venture is the dolphins' lack of fear of man.

Perhaps the ancient legend of the boy and the dolphin is not so far-fetched as it might seem. According to this story, a small boy befriended a dolphin and fed it. In return, it carried him on its back across the water. They became close companions and felt great love for one another. Several years later the boy fell sick and died: his animal friend was distraught. The story concludes, 'The dolphin gave not over his haunt, but usually came to the wonted place, and missing the lad, seemed to be heavy and mourn again, until for very grief and sorrow, he also was found dead upon the shore.'

This may be no more than a legend, but great love is possible between human and other animals, and we can encounter dolphins at close quarters in the wild. Why, then, should we want them to jump through hoops and perform funny tricks? If we want to enjoy interaction with animals in our human world, perhaps it is best to concentrate our efforts most on the tame species that can no longer exist in nature because of the way we have modified them: the animals we call pets.

*　　　*　　　*

Pet-keeping is not, as many people imagine, a modern phenomenon resulting from the affluence of advanced countries: it is an ancient and deeply entrenched facet of human society.

Anthropologists have repeatedly discovered that tribal societies with primitive technology nearly always demonstrate some kind of pet-keeping. This is not confined to childless women, or to children. It is a common and widespread practice. American Indians, when they were first encountered, were found to be harbouring all kinds of companion animals, not for gain but simply for fun. They kept tame moose, bison, wolves and bears. When young, some of these animals were even breast-fed by the women of the tribes.

The Indians also kept birds and were shocked at the suggestion that these might be good to eat: indeed, they refused to eat pet birds even when they belonged to species that were otherwise regularly consumed. Once an individual animal had become a pet it was no longer a stranger, but a wordless friend to be treated as one of the family, sharing the home and being cared for as if it were as important as a human. The American Indians were not unusual in this respect. Similar reactions were found among South Sea islanders, Australian Aborigines, Andaman Islanders and Bornean Dyaks.

The variety of animals observed in tribal homes around the world is staggering: everything from lizards and parrots to pigs and monkeys were kept as pets. Usually they were brought back from the hunt by tribesmen and given to their children as playthings. The young animals then grew up in the home and became companions for the whole family. Regardless of affluence or poverty, of age or sex, of primitive social conditions or advanced technology, of down-to-earth practicality or decadent sentimentality, pet-keeping has been popular right across the human spectrum and almost as widespread as religion. For most of us today, however, there are only two pets with which we are prepared to share our homes and gardens: the cat and the dog are the only two species of animal ever to be given the full freedom of our houses.

Domestic pets have been bred for generations to adapt them as much as possible to our way of life. Reared from birth in our presence, they become 'bilingual': as much at ease with us as with their own kind, and able to enjoy both types of relationship.

The Animal Contract that exists between man and dog is about as ideal as it can get. For their human companions, dogs provide many rewards. For example, pet-owners live longer, on average, than those without pets. It seems that the dogs' lively but soothing presence acts as a de-stressing device for harassed urbanites. Pet-owners who were wired up experimentally to test their physiological responses showed a rapid and significant calming after only a few moments of caressing their favourite pet animal. Heart-attack patients are less likely to experience a second attack if they own a dog or a cat. Pet-owners are undeniably healthier than pet-haters. Pets also provide emotional rewards, acting as pseudo-children and satisfying our often-frustrated parental urges.

The good news for pets is that, at the very least, they do not have to be displayed to paying customers, nor are they part of a huge collection of animals. Being personally owned they receive more individual attention. The main drawback of being a pet is that your owner may be unaware of your precise needs: pet-owners, despite their very best intentions, can be ignorant and may even kill with kindness. Another disadvantage of being a pet is that the motivation of the owner is often flawed. Instead of wishing simply to celebrate the pet as a member of another species, the owner wishes to use it to satisfy some human need: the need for a baby, a child, or an obedient subordinate. The result is that the pet may find itself over-mothered or over-disciplined. Such are the shortcomings of being a pet, but none of them is inevitable. It is entirely possible for a pet animal to live out its life in an almost ideal way, with all its natural behaviour patterns gaining full expression while at the same time its medical problems are dealt with efficiently: the best of both worlds, and a good contract for all concerned.

Despite the spreading urbanisation which makes pet-keeping more difficult, the popularity of both cats and dogs shows no sign of declining. Indeed it is actually on the increase. In Britain a few years ago a survey revealed that there were 5.7 million dogs and 5.2 million cats; now both these figures have risen above the 6 million mark. In the United States there were 35 million cats and 48 million dogs; now there are 56.2 million cats and 51 million dogs. Not only are both species gaining in popularity, but cats are starting to outnumber dogs for the first time. The reason is obvious: the needs of dogs are less easily adapted to city living and there is more and more city in which the pets have to live. Even so there is one dog for every ten Britons and one dog for every five Americans – a striking testimony in these modern times to the huge appeal of the canine companion. Worldwide they must be among the most numerous and therefore the most successful of all non-human animals.

Their success is due to the extent to which, after thousands of years of domestication, they have come to accept our way of life as theirs. They do this by becoming, in effect, split personalities, leading double lives. In part of their brains they are adult cats or dogs, encountering their kind, arguing, mating and rearing their young. In another part of their brains they remain forever infantile, always kittens or puppies in their dealings with us. We remain their pseudo-parents throughout their long lives and they treat us, more or less, with proper parental respect. This double existence is what gives pet cats and dogs their special charm, for we can feel dominant to them, as parents, and at the same time enjoy their company as adult animals.

Their appeal has become so immense that there are now over 50 breeds of cat and over 400 breeds of dog. As pedigree animals they are shown competitively right around the world from Sydney to San Francisco and from Moscow to Manchester.

The first major cat show was held in 1871, and the first dog show a little earlier, in 1859. They were an immediate success and special clubs and societies were formed to organise them in the years that followed. Today there are thousands of such shows every year and they serve to standardise the breeds and maintain a high level of expertise in the care and keeping of these animals.

Dog shows, in particular, have become huge events with as many as 15,000 animals being brought together to compete with one another in the show ring. For those people participating, the shows are important occasions and are taken very seriously. For those outside the highly specialised world of pedigree dogs, these events have often been the subject of ridicule. They are rarely shown seriously on television as sporting competitions.

The critics of dog shows argue that the dogs are being exploited in the show ring by their intensely competitive owners who are greedy for glory even if it is at the expense of the animals' comforts. Dog shows are an easy target, but what are the facts? Contrary to critical opinion, the dogs love these occasions. The travelling with their owners, the rich landscape of canine fragrances when they arrive, the bustle and the excitement, and the very complexity of it all are elements that, for the highly sociable dog, make a good substitute for a primeval pack-hunting expedition. The shows break the monotony of the ordinary daily routine in a manner that is well suited to the canine personality. The competitiveness of the shows ensures that standards of canine health and care are extremely high.

Pedigree dogs may irritate some puritans because of the amount of fuss and attention they get, but the truth is that these dogs are among the luckiest of all our four-legged companions. If anyone suffers in this Animal Contract it is surely the owners rather than the dogs.

One of the criticisms against showing dogs is that pedigree breeds have been taken too far in the search for champions. This has been vigorously denied by dog-breeders. It only applies to a few breeds, where the back has become too long, the skin too loose, or the face too flat. In each of these cases careful breeding programmes are now under way to correct the faults. Until this has been successfully achieved, the whole of the pedigree-dog world will be vulnerable to accusations of callous indifference and it is not surprising that, in a cultural atmosphere of increasing sensitivity to issues of animal welfare, the breeders are seeking to put their house in order.

Another criticism concerns the continued use of unnecessary mutilations for purposes of show-style. Some dogs have their ears trimmed to give them a sharp, pointed outline; others have their tails amputated to give them the fashionable docked appearance traditional for their breed. The Council of Europe has now banned these two medieval practices and they should soon disappear as a result.

Whatever the criticisms, today's pedigree dog can reasonably expect to live a long life of canine luxury. Compared with the benefits they enjoy, the disadvantages of their association with mankind are trivial.

Some pet-owners take on tasks that seem daunting even to the most enthusiastic animal-lovers. This may be to do with the sheer numbers kept, or with the species chosen. An English schoolboy persuaded his long-suffering parents to permit him to fill their front room with over 1000 cockroaches, of many different species, carefully collected from all over the world. A lady from the north of England started a tortoise hotline to rescue unwanted pets of this type and save them from early deaths. In her small semi-detached house she now cares for over 100 hungry tortoises, each of which is taken upstairs to sleep at night in special dormitories. During the daytime they form a living carpet downstairs, awaiting their feeding time, when mountains of fruit and vegetables are brought in on trays and distributed about the floor. The entire house revolves around the devoted care of these reptiles.

For other people, something more dramatic is needed. The keeping of large, dangerous and potentially lethal animals such as gorillas, bears, lions and tigers, or highly poisonous ones such as snakes, has a special appeal for a particular kind of pet-owner. Perhaps they wish to test their own courage while at the same time enjoying the proximity of spectacular animals. The daily escape from the jaws of death is a special reward, an endlessly repeated risk that excites the human ego. In addition there is the reward of proving that close friendships can exist even with potentially dangerous species, and the challenge of trying to destroy the myths and bad reputations surrounding them.

All too often in the past the savagery of such animals has been caused by the brutal way they have been treated by humans rather than by some inherent viciousness in their characters. The 'savage beast' is largely the invention of the cowardly big-game hunter, propagated to make him seem brave. To the expert pet-keeper who specialises in large animals, the big-game hunter is a bad joke. To him the bear, the wolf, the lion or the gorilla is a member of the family and the achievement of proving that, given the right conditions, such creatures are naturally friendly is justification enough for keeping them in somewhat artificial conditions. These animals, playing with their owners or simply sharing their quarters, are good advertisements for their species, reminding all of us that the old images of 'evil, savage monsters' are fictions born out of fear, ignorance and superstition.

The keeping of exotic pets polarises the experts. Some see it as a way of saving animals such as the tiger from almost certain extinction in the wild; others see it as the unhappy creation of a mental hybrid, an animal that is tamed but not domesticated, a humanised tiger that cannot return to the wild and yet cannot live freely in human society like its domestic counterparts.

For some animals, like the gorilla, the natural environment has become so hazardous that even an artificial forest may be preferable. In the south of England a collection of gorillas is housed in vast enclosures, which their owner enters every day in order to play with the animals and retain his role as a member of their society. To date the worst he has suffered is a broken finger, snapped in the jaws of the biggest male gorilla on a day when the animal was more interested in a nearby female than in his human friend. Despite their tameness with their owner, they continue to breed normally and successfully. Thirty gorillas have been bred – a record that makes major zoos look highly inefficient. Like dogs, they survive the split personality that sees them as part human and part ape. Time and again ambitious pet-owners like this are showing that the old images of bloodthirsty monsters are simply fairy tales, dating from the time when we were instructed by the Church to subdue and dominate all of nature.

Many of us have a strong desire to keep pets of one kind or another, but if we do so we are entering a contract that requires considerable sacrifice on our part. Good pet-keepers quickly discover that their lives are taken over by their animals and they soon become fanatics, spending more and more time, money and ingenuity in solving the problems that pets create.

It is almost impossible to honour this type of Animal Contract without this obsessive process taking place. The casual pet-keeper is nearly always a bad one.

Providing they are intelligently cared for, pets provide a massive reward for their owners. Through these animals the humans involved are constantly reminded of their kinship with other forms of life. With this reminder comes, almost unconsciously, a realisation that we are all part of an evolved family sharing one very small and highly vulnerable planet. Every intimate exchange with a pet animal brings home to us that we too are animals, and not some magically protected beings for whom the laws of nature do not apply. By reminding us that we are part of nature, our pets help to warn us that if we ignore our humble origins we may easily be on the road to extinction.

Despite all the advantages, both for the animals and their owners, there are those individuals who are intensely hostile to the whole idea of keeping pet dogs and cats. They attempt to increase the restrictions on pet-keeping in all cities and to drive all forms of animal life out of our major human population areas. Their excuse is nearly always a matter of hygiene, but behind their campaigns lurks something more sinister: a fear of their own role in nature. They wish to distance themselves totally from natural processes and isolate themselves from the biological reality of which they are a part. If they ever succeed we are in danger of losing our understanding of our own animal nature. That way lies environmental disaster: a world without animals, made up only of man and machines.

*　　*　　*

The world would be a tidier and cleaner place without our animal companions around us. Life would be simpler and we would be guilt-free, unable to inflict even accidental discomfort upon them. City-dwellers could dispense with animals altogether, and country folk merely glance at them from a distance. However, the loss of intimacy would quickly lead to a new kind of abuse: the loss of interest. To understand this it is only necessary to look at what has happened already to the more remote forms of wildlife.

Many fascinating species of wildlife are on the verge of extinction and the list of animals that are likely to vanish for ever during the twenty-first century is depressingly long. Many people are concerned about this impending disaster but few of those who care deeply have the political power to do anything about it. Those who do have power are too preoccupied with pressing human problems to be prepared to give priority to other species.

Many conservation bodies have been formed and many brave and sometimes brilliant salvage operations have been mounted to rescue a particular species or a local habitat, but when they are all added together they amount to little more than the administration of a soothing ointment to someone who is suffering from the plague. Viewed globally, the battle to save the world's wildlife is being lost on a scale so grand that an objective observer from another planet would see little hope for the long-term future.

For centuries Europeans have been gradually but systematically decimating their own wildlife, setting an example that was later to be followed by the countries they colonised. A thousand years ago there were wild bears and wolves roaming Britain, and wild animals of many kinds were plentiful across the beautiful wooded countryside of all European countries.

By the eighteenth century, the landscape had been transformed into a neat patchwork of rectangular fields. The countryside was being cleaned up and cultivated to provide food for the growing population. The wild areas were dramatically reduced. During the industrial revolution the urban centres began to grow like patches of fungus, eating up more and more of the land. Finally, the twentieth-century farmers started to use pesticides, poisoning the prey on which so many of the remaining larger forms of wildlife depended. The taming of the countryside was almost complete. Throughout all this the gentry were hunting, shooting and fishing for sport, while the poachers took their leftovers for the pot. In retrospect it is surprising that we have any wildlife left at all.

Not content with destroying wild Europe, our ancestors travelled to foreign parts to kill more exotic fauna. Sporting guns were soon shooting big game in Africa, India, South America and anywhere else that the bewildered beasts would stand still long enough to make an easy target. With increasingly sophisticated weapons it was a one-sided competition, and the walls of European houses were soon groaning under the weight of stuffed animal heads.

The local people watched this slaughter and came to the conclusion that, to be truly civilised, it was necessary to shoot every animal in sight. They did their best to follow suit. We had taught them well. Big-game hunters were not the only models for them to observe. Throughout the Victorian period many naturalist explorers joined in the kill, as they went about the business of building up vast collections of museum specimens, skulls and skins.

The wild areas of the world were so extensive and the wild animals so numerous that the killing did not seem to matter. It could only make a small dent, surely, in the fauna of the world. However, almost unnoticed, something else was taking place: human populations everywhere were on the increase. They had to be fed and more land had to be taken into cultivation. Even in such remote places as the 'Dark Continent' of Africa, the wild places began to shrink. Yet as recently as the first half of the twentieth century, the alarm bells failed to ring. It was not until after the Second World War that a few far-seeing individuals began to feel uneasy. They guessed that as the colonies became independent they would behave more and more like their old colonial masters, and do to their own wilds what Europeans had done to Europe. Somehow they had to be convinced that, unlike the occupants of the so-called advanced countries, they must treat their wildlife with respect. Clearly this would not be an easy trick to pull off.

Special organisations were formed to help with this task. The International Union for the Conservation of Nature (IUCN) dates from 1956 and the World Wildlife Fund, now the World Wide Fund for Nature (WWF), from 1961. Since it was difficult to adopt a high moral tone, the poachers-turned-gamekeepers adopted a strategy based on practical considerations. Instead of arguing that animals should be conserved for their own sake, they concentrated on the idea that they should be protected because of their usefulness. If the wild fauna thrived it could help a country economically and perhaps even scientifically. The animals could be exploited as a tourist attraction, as a source of food, or as a source of important medicines.

This argument was well received by the less-advanced countries, who recognised the force of economic factors. They had been taught the importance of these by the advanced countries they had come to admire and imitate. Practical conservation swung into action, and there were some immediate triumphs. The magnificent game parks welcomed privileged tourists to their newly built safari lodges. The visitors shot the wildlife not with guns but with cameras, and went home happy with the thought that the local people were not, after all, going to behave as badly as Europeans.

This was true so long as the animals could be exploited without killing them. If they could attract badly needed foreign currency simply by being stared at, like cageless zoo animals, they were safe. Big-game hunting was severely restricted in many places and outlawed altogether in others. The tourists flocked in. Today, the wild animals in certain parts of Africa are more likely to suffer from exhaust fumes than from gunshot wounds. At dawn each day swarms of trucks, zebra-striped mini-vans and Land-Rovers spread out from the safari lodges in search of prize sightings. Bristling with telescopic lenses, they bump and lurch in all directions, like bees searching for pollen. Within minutes of being spotted, a sleeping lion finds itself surrounded by a dozen vehicles. They jostle for position, like the royalty-watching ratpack searching for the best photograph. If the lion suddenly feels a pang of hunger and decides to set off on a hunt, he is eagerly followed every step of the way by an impatient tourist armada. At the sight of this rapidly approaching traffic jam, all potential prey animals scatter in panic. The lion goes hungry.

Cheetah suffer most and it is now estimated that tourist pollution is the main cause of the dramatic decline in their numbers. A mother cheetah with cubs is never left alone, from dawn until dusk. The cubs need regular food, but she cannot provide it for them. In desperation, some predators have abandoned their natural behaviour patterns and switched to nocturnal hunting, to avoid the rush hour that lasts all day. Leopards are harassed in the same way and are also becoming increasingly rare. With new safari lodges being built every month, the future looks even more crowded.

Our carefully conserved wildlife is also under threat from the local people. Their population figures make startling reading. In Kenya, for example, the average number of children per family is eight and a half. That country, which boasts some of the finest wildlife on the face of the earth, also has the highest population growth rate ever recorded for any country in the world. All around the game parks, local people are gathering, demanding more farming land and more living space. Each year, the authorities are forced to trim another 5 per cent off this park, another 10 per cent off that one. It is never enough, and some of the local people are driven to desperate measures. They become poachers.

In some areas poaching has reached epidemic proportions. In Tsavo Game Park, for instance, over 40,000 of the 45,000 elephants have been killed by poachers in the last ten years. Arming the game wardens has done little to help. Large gangs with machine-guns now attack at night, armed with torches and chain-saws. They have been known to slaughter as many as six rhino in one attack, sawing off their horns – worth even more than elephant tusks – in a matter of seconds. Any animal that has great commercial value is vulnerable. The ghosts of the early European plunderers still haunt the land.

All over Africa the story is much the same. It has been calculated that, at the end of the Second World War, African wildlife had only one-tenth of the living space that it enjoyed in Victorian times. Forty years later, in the mid-1980s, it had been further reduced to one-tenth of one-tenth. In other words, what we see today is only one-hundredth of what was witnessed by early Victorian naturalists. Where does this leave our grandchildren?

To answer this it is necessary to consider the curious breeding habits of the human species. We appear to have established a new principle that can be summed up as follows: the wilder your country, the faster you reproduce. Industrialised countries, despite all their medical care, advanced hygiene and improved diets, are now increasing their populations at only a very moderate rate. At present it would take Western Europe 436 years to double its population. The populations of less urbanised countries increase much faster: the doubling time in the USSR, for example, is 83 years. The populations of undeveloped countries, with great expanses of wild land and dramatic wild fauna, increase faster still: the doubling time in Asia is 36 years; in Latin America 30 years; and in Africa – still the treasure house of the world's most exciting fauna – a staggeringly low 23 years.

At present there are about 500 million people living in Africa. The population of Europe is roughly the same. In a quarter of a century the number of people in Africa will at least have doubled: an additional 500 million people will have to find somewhere to live. This is the equivalent of taking the entire population of present-day Europe and shipping it to Africa, settling the people in new homes there and feeding them.

In a mere quarter of a century, Africa will have lost most of its wild places, partly in housing and partly in new farming land, to feed the new towns. In half a century it will, like all the wild places of the world, have become a highly urbanised, highly industrialised continent. Jungles, wild grasslands, swamps and woodlands will all have vanished. The great game parks will have shrunk to local zoos. The process is already gaining momentum.

The plight of the elephant highlights the dilemma. The elephant population of Africa is halved each decade. In 1979 it stood at 1.3 million; by 1988 it had sunk to 740,000. In some countries poachers are accelerating this decline; ironically, in countries where poaching has been eradicated, the slaughter continues, but this time with official blessing. The elephants' problem is that they now seem to breed either too much or too little: we have upset the balance of nature. If they are allowed to breed freely they quickly eat themselves out of house and home, lay waste the landscape and starve slowly to death. To prevent this, the conservationists have to revert to the earlier role of big-game hunters and crop or cull – that is to say, massacre – the herds.

In Uganda, between 1924 and 1969, the Game Department butchered the amazing total of 46,000 elephants. And in Zimbabwe, even today, in one game park alone, hundreds have to be rounded up and killed each year by game rangers with machine-guns. The slaughter is terrible to behold and is certainly not the picture that is presented when the conservationists are begging for funds to help them save the world's precious heritage of wild animals.

It begins with a helicopter flight. In a matter of minutes a herd is sighted. There together are the elderly matriarchs, the breeding cows, a few young males, some half-grown calves and a number of babies. The helicopter circles this typical elephant herd of 20–30 animals, driving them in panic into a tight bunch. Then it lands and men with machine-guns spread out. On a signal they start firing, killing the entire group, even the smallest babies. The sound of the guns is exceeded by the screaming of the animals as they are hit, or as they see their companions hit. The noise is unbelievable, but it does not last long. It only takes 45 seconds to slaughter a large herd. Then, as an eye-witness reports, 'All that was left was a great pile of carcasses. And there was so much silence. Then I did hear something else. It was like a little creek running, a little gurgling. I looked at the big pile of elephants that had been so crowded together that some had fallen on top of each other. There were fountains of blood rushing out and running down the carcasses. That was what caused the gurgling. And that lasted a couple of minutes or so. Then . . . I went away and sat under a tree.'

This particular observer was so shaken by what he had seen that he could no longer support such a programme. He asked the heart-searching question, 'Do we really have to start perpetrating scenes like that on a large scale . . . just because it suits the exigencies of human populations . . . Is that what we have to do?'

His agony is caused by the certain knowledge that, if they are allowed to overpopulate, the elephants will suffer a much more horrible and prolonged death from gradual starvation. Why should this happen? Surely this cannot be the natural pattern of life for elephants? Of course it is not. The African elephant population had, over millions of years, reached a state of stability. Minor predation by large carnivores and by prehistoric human hunters using spears and primitive traps kept the numbers at a reasonable level. Later on, big-game hunters took over the role of predators. Then the human populations began to swell and the natural range of the elephants shrank. They became overcrowded and the problems began. Conservationists started to reduce their numbers systematically, to fit their reduced circumstances. In Uganda, for example, in 1924 the elephants had 75 per cent of the land.

By 1969 this had dwindled to only 13 per cent. Little wonder that the Game Department had to kill so many thousands of them. There was no choice.

For those kind-hearted individuals who strive to rescue captive animals and return them to the peace and quiet of the wild, this does not make happy reading. If you happen to be an African elephant it appears to be a case of 'if the poachers don't get you, the conservationists will'. In a recent book on the horrors of animal life in captivity there is a photograph of an elephant with its baby in Africa, with the caption, 'The beauty and dignity of the wild.' Would that it were so.

Africa is not the only area that faces disaster. All over the world, the tropical rain forests are being felled for development. In the past 40 years they have been reduced to a mere half of their former area. Eleven million acres are being flattened every year. That is 20 acres a minute, every minute, day and night, every year, year after year. Fifty per cent of all the known species of plants and animals on the planet are found in these tropical forests and it is estimated that, at the present rate of forest destruction, one animal species becomes extinct every day. Worse still, the climate control afforded by these once-vast forests is being lost. The world is getting warmer. White Christmases are a thing of the past and before too long the polar ice-caps will start melting. The oceans will rise and all the great coastal cities, such as London and New York, will find themselves submerged. Perhaps then, at last, someone in power will decide to act. It seems a pity to wait that long.

Why has the conservation movement not had greater impact? The answer lies with the people involved with it. To put it bluntly, they are too gentle and too polite. They have played safe. They have concentrated on short-term tactics instead of calmly considering long-term strategies. They have played on the emotions of rich urbanites who are remote from the real issues in order to raise funds. They have done this by focusing on the plight of the most appealing animal failures. Nothing produces such a glow of human kindness (or, if one is being unpleasantly objective, of smug superiority) as offering help to an attractive failure. To gain this aid an animal should be cuddly, attractively coloured, extremely rare, or better still all three. As top losers, giant pandas are obvious winners. Successful rodents need not apply.

The first rule of conservation, therefore, became the protection of nice animals on the verge of extinction; the nasty ones could look after themselves. In other words, it was pest control in reverse. To a zoologist this seems a highly dubious principle: if an animal has to be a failure in order to be interesting, there is something wrong. Yet, time and again, conservationists put all their efforts into assisting species on the verge of extinction. These animals have become the stars of the conservation show and converted it into an elitist game.

What is missing is an underlying philosophy that can guide the movement. It is a movement that has to achieve that most difficult of all feats: the shifting of public opinion away from an entrenched attitude. That attitude is rooted in the ancient totem animals and also in the good and evil animals of medieval times. It embodies the idea that some animals are nice and others are nasty. Human thinking has been riddled with this fallacy for centuries and something special is needed to dislodge it.

Every animal, every single living species, is the fascinating end-point of millions of years of evolution. Each is uniquely adapted to its own way of life and each deserves our respect. What the conservation movement has failed to grasp is that each animal has to be valued for what it is, not for what it is worth. Each animal must be honoured for its own sake, regardless of its prettiness, rarity or monetary value. Until it is understood that the common house sparrow is as wonderful and as mysterious as the rarest bird of paradise, there will be little hope for the future. Until we have achieved this state of mind we will always be prone to view nature in a mirror distorted by our own selfishness and our irrational personal biases. We will squander our conservational energies on emotionally charged rescue operations and will ignore the more global problems that beset us.

If we are to share the planet with other animals, we must do so in an impartial way. We must find ways of standing back and letting the natural relations between the species operate. If we interfere we will become what one author has aptly called the Gardeners of Eden, deciding which animals are blooms and which are weeds. That job is beyond us, as harassed conservationists are already discovering to their cost. They call it wildlife management and it is so full of pitfalls that only blind optimists would attempt it. To be fair, they cannot be blamed for trying, because they are confronted with so many desperate local situations. It is impossible to ignore these, any more than someone can stop scratching at sores when suffering from a major disease. The ointment of wildlife management may soothe the irritations, but it does not cure the disease.

Conservation has gone astray because it has failed to confront the disease that is causing all the trouble. The organisers of the movement have been too embarrassed to face the simple truth: if human breeding is not restricted, wildlife will disappear. As long as they fail to address this issue, everything they do will prove to be cosmetic and trivial. They may win the battle to save the giant panda, but they will lose the war of the world. It will prove a Pyrrhic victory.

It is not surprising that the conservationists have shirked this central issue. It is a tricky subject. On the surface it suggests putting animals before babies. What is worse, it means putting African animals before African babies and Indian animals before Indian babies. This is frightening because it starts to make conservationism look anti-human, favouring the beasts over the people. No wonder the issue has been sidestepped so many times.

Other solutions have been sought. It has been pointed out that there are many ways in which wasteful anti-animal practices can be corrected where there is no conflict between man and animal. We can find ways of sharing our developed land with animals more successfully. We can redevelop land that is being inefficiently used, so that we do not have to take further virgin lands away from other animals, and we can look for non-animal substitutes for animal products wherever possible. These are all useful measures, but in the end they will simply not be enough. The explosion of human populations will swamp everything.

Politicians are no help here. Tacitly or openly, they all follow what has been called the Creed of the Cancer Cell: the economic philosophy of the need for perpetual growth. Every politician talks about the need for 'more hospitals, more schools, more industry, more housing', as though more is inevitably, unquestionably, an improvement for society. For some reason deeply embedded in the power-wielding mentality of cultural leaders, it seems impossible to see the advantage of asking for fewer people in better hospitals, better schools and better houses. The human species is not a high-quantity species, biologically speaking: it is a high-quality one. There is nothing but misery to be gained from gross overpopulation and that is why the conservationists need not be worried about asking for fewer babies in order to make room for other species. This would not be an anti-human persecution of the pre-industrial countries: it would be a great gift to them if only they could accept the idea. The developing countries' true affluence lies not in bulging, half-starved masses, but in carefully limited populations. They must be helped to realise that, just because some countries have made mistakes and have overpopulated, there is no glory in following in their stupid footsteps. They must be persuaded to accept that their own countries have unique qualities as the last sanctuaries of one of the world's greatest spectacles: its wildlife roaming free. They must be convinced that they need much larger game parks, not smaller ones, where the animals can continue to enjoy their natural habitats without the need for game management and where the tourist density will not be too obtrusive.

The conservation movement must come out of the closet and declare itself totally behind human population control.

II

Fair Game?

Fair Game?

Man evolved as a hunter: a tribal hunter preying on large animals. In modern cities it is easy to find food without owning a spear but for a million years success in the hunt was a matter of survival: hunting moulded our human personality.

The city has often been called a concrete jungle, but in reality it is more like a human zoo, its overcrowded inhabitants held captive by the environment they have built for themselves. What would happen if one of these human-zoo inmates was returned to the wild, stripped of clothing, implements, instruments, vehicles and all the other trappings of civilisation, and placed back in the primeval grasslands where he evolved? He would soon come face to face with the fact that he is not after all a fallen angel but a risen ape, and indeed a very naked ape: just another animal whose only remarkable feature is his over-sized brain.

His most pressing problem would be finding food. Lacking sharp claws or fangs, he would have to use his cunning to defeat his prey: a case of talent instead of talons. He would also need help from his friends, involving tribal co-operation and group organisation. With brains, weapons and mutual aid he could survive.

In the age of the supermarket these problems seem utterly

remote. It has become easy for us to find food today. The animals we hunt on the supermarket shelves are neatly packaged, canned and wrapped, so that they hardly seem like real prey that have been killed for our consumption. Many of them bear no visual resemblance to the living organisms they once were. As chunks, slabs and slices they are distanced from the hunt, the chase, and the kill.

How has this shift affected our attitudes? What has happened to the primordial hunter within us? Where have our urges to pursue and catch our prey been sublimated? How has our new pattern of feeding changed our views about animals?

For something like a million years our ancestors treated other animals in a simple, straightforward manner: they hunted prey, avoided predators, repelled pests, and attacked parasites. They did not go out of their way to persecute other creatures: in their terms that would have been wasteful and pointless. They killed and ate only what they needed in order to survive, and they destroyed only those life forms that threatened their well-being. Their response to other animals was very different from ours. In many ways they considered them their equals or superiors. Many animals had faster legs, a better sense of smell, stronger teeth and more acute hearing. Our ancestors were right to respect them.

At that stage there was a very simple contract between mankind and other animals. It stated: if our bellies are full and you cause us no harm, we will leave you in peace. It was perhaps a one-sided arrangement, but not wantonly cruel or excessive. We offered them the chance to live out their lives without interference unless we were hungry; we took from them their flesh but only when we were actually hungry.

The essential point here is that, although we killed animals to survive, they were able to live out a full, natural existence in the wild state before their deaths. We may have caused those deaths, but we did not interfere with the animals' way of life before that moment. In this respect we were behaving just like any other predatory species. Where we differed was in using our brains rather than our brawn. It was our success in the hunt that shaped our human personalities. Not only did hunting make us more co-operative than our monkey relatives, but we also became more bipedal, freeing our grasping hands to be put to a thousand new uses. The handling of weapons and implements became second nature to us.

Growing out of the hunting lifestyle was a new pattern of reproduction, with the arrival of pair-bonds, the loss of the breeding season, the development of strong territoriality, the division of labour, and above all the advent of spoken language. It also made us superstitious and our simple superstitions eventually became complex religions. All of this resulted from one simple switch in feeding, from fruit-gathering to hunting. It was a major transformation that set us on our human pathway to global success.

There are two essential differences between vegetation-eaters and meat-eaters. In the first place, it takes far longer to collect and consume enough of the bulky, inferior vegetable diet to sustain a healthy body. Vegetation-eaters like gorillas have little spare time to do anything other than feed. They start feeding as soon as they wake up in the morning and continue until their midday siesta, after which they feed again until they bed down for the night. Other activities – fighting, mating, playing, dealing with enemies – are merely brief interruptions in the long daily grind of monotonous plant-chewing. By contrast, meat-eaters can kill and consume their highly nutritious food in a fraction of the time, leaving themselves leisure for other activities. For a python this means a great deal of time to sleep and digest, but for people it means time to be creative and imaginative. The simple device of increasing our meat intake gave us the opportunity to turn our minds to higher things.

The second difference is connected with the way food is obtained. Vegetation-eaters have no need to co-operate. They are not forced to surround a plum or overpower a berry in order to eat it. They do not have to discuss the tactics required to sneak up on an apple, or trap a walnut. There is no pressing need for co-operation and communication. For the meat-eater the development of these skills is vital. Meat-eating gave us our increased urges to help one another and to debate our shared dilemmas.

The great benefits we gained as a result of our new diet did not, however, necessitate a complete change. We only had to increase the meat element in our diet from a minor to a major part. All monkeys and apes are minor meat-eaters, taking insects, small birds, eggs and other form of animal life in their normal daily diet; and all humans, even Eskimos, take at least a little vegetable food in theirs. However, the shift from eating a little meat to eating a lot was enough to set us on our astonishingly successful evolutionary trajectory.

During the million years of hunting we went through some physiological changes. Our digestive system adapted to the new regime, ensuring that we never slipped back into the time-consuming monotony of the vegetation-eater. Our infants developed an extremely high protein need – as much as four times that of adults. This means that for the growing child a meatless diet would in most instances be disastrous and would result in a rapid decline in the local population.

Furthermore, in both children and adults, there appear to have been genetic changes that effectively forced human populations to maintain a meat diet or perish. According to biomedical experts we now lack whole sets of genes needed for the production of eight essential amino acids. We can only obtain these in a simple way from meat, which contains them in the perfect balance for our digestive systems. Plant food may contain one or other of them, but they are useless if taken singly. Indeed, they must all be ingested at the same time if they are to work. It is only necessary for one of them to be missing from a meal for all the others to be useless. This looks like another evolutionary safeguard, ensuring that we keep to our meat diet, and avoid backsliding to the world of herbivores.

The primeval hunting tribes, in which the males brought home the meat and the females gathered roots and berries to create a simple, mixed, primal diet, probably had few problems of nutrition other than the occasional brief period of hunger. We think of those faraway days as dull and brutish, but the truth is likely to have been rather different. Already intensely co-operative, the prehistoric hunter was a sensitive, intelligent and remarkably successful individual. On his own terms he was affluent. The entire human population in the Old Stone Age has been estimated at between only 2 and 3 million people. There was plenty of land for everyone, game was plentiful and our hunting ranges must have seemed boundless. It must have been a good time to live, despite the crude images we have been given of that distant, formative era.

Then, as recently as 10,000 years ago, our hunting ancestors took a small but momentous step. They started to cultivate crops. This gave them the additional affluence of a food surplus which they could store. The hunter was about to be eclipsed by a new kind of human being: the farmer.

Inevitably, the farmers' crops attracted uninvited guests.

Herbivores arrived to graze on them and became serious pests. In due course, however, the farmers realised that they could trap these animals and put them to work helping to grow the crops. The animals could also be kept for their milk and killed if necessary for their meat and hides. The crops were now not only providing food for the human settlements, but were also attracting meat to the sites. There was no longer any need to hunt: the prey was coming to the predator and animal husbandry was beginning.

It was this development that finally led the majority of mankind over the threshold from a hunting life to a farming life: the decision to keep wild animals in captivity and let them breed there under human control, for generation after generation, all the time selecting stock that was more docile and better at supplying meat, milk or whatever products they could offer. A new Animal Contract was forged: the animals gave us their labour, their meat, their milk and their hides, and we gave them food, shelter and protection from predators.

This switch from hunting to farming forced us to become more settled. We were tied to particular places by the need to look after our carefully cultivated plots of land. Hunters had always worked from a home base, but this base could be moved whenever the game moved. The farmer, having invested so much time in taming his fields, was more sedentary. This brought its own problems. He may have enjoyed a food store and a food surplus, but he was vulnerable to local disasters: drought or flooding could destroy the harvest; disease could decimate his livestock.

In some Third World areas today, the farmer still lives on the edge of survival. He and his animals thrive or perish together and the bond between these farmers and their animals is a major feature of their existence. Man and animal depend on one another for their survival. Modern man living in an industrial age can hardly conceive of the importance of this bond. It is a benign contract involving a close personal rapport between the farmer and his stock. This is a relationship stretching back for at least 8000 years, to the time when cattle were first domesticated.

We know something about the domestication of livestock from the study of animal bones left on settlement sites in the Middle East, the cradle of civilisation. Ten thousand years ago there were cultivated crops – wheat and barley – but the animal bones at this very early stage were still those of hunted animals such as gazelles and, surprisingly, foxes. Then, about 9000 years ago, this pattern changed: goats and sheep were being eaten, and domesticated food had arrived. A thousand years later cattle and pigs had been added to the human farmyard. A whole new way of life had begun and the basic family of farm animals was firmly established.

We know that is what happened, but why did it happen? Hunting and collecting berries were easier than tilling the fields, harvesting cereals, grinding them up, preparing them, and then feeding the captive prey as well, instead of letting them feed themselves as wild animals before hunting and killing them. There were to be advantages once the farming system had been instituted – the advantages of food to spare and the avoidance of uncertainties and periods of hunger – but what triggered the movement in the first place, before those advantages had become apparent? Why switch from uncomplicated hunting to the fatigue of farming?

The answer is that there were already too many people: the human race was proving too much of a success. The numbers of the species were increasing and there were more and more mouths to feed for a given hunting area. We were breeding so fast and spreading so far that the simple hunt could no longer sustain us. In some areas the game animals were starting to dwindle in number. We had to find a way of producing food in large quantities. It was easy enough to store crops: we could construct grain-stores and keep the cereals safe for later use. It was more difficult to store meat because it went bad and we had not yet discovered methods of preserving it by smoking and drying. Despite the extra work entailed in keeping animals fed and housed, the living larder, domesticated stock, was the only answer.

In taking this great step, mankind was making a move backwards in behaviour. From the daring, inventive hunter, with time to laugh and play between hunts, man had turned himself into a drudge. The repetitive lifestyle of the early farmer lacked all the excitements of the chase and returned him to an almost bovine condition as far as behaviour was concerned. He still ate a mixed diet of meat and vegetables – the omnivorous diet to which he had adapted his gut during a million years of slow evolution – but now he obtained it in ways as dull and routine as anything faced by the primitive plant-eaters from which he had diverged in his primeval, pre-human days.

This was a long-term problem he had to solve, but first there was a more immediate challenge. Animals were not the only thieves attracted to the settled farms. Nomadic tribespeople arrived and stole the domestic animals they found so conveniently penned, leading to a fascinating split: those domestic animals that could be herded and driven from place to place became the typical stock of the pastoralists, while those that could not be driven were closely linked to the settled farmers. Cattle, sheep and goats could be driven, but pigs could not and they became hated by the pastoralists as symbolising their enemies, the settled farmers. Later cultures that grew out of the nomadic, pastoral tribesmen consistently hated pork, and the Semitic peoples – the Jews and Muslims – who descended from the early pastoral, nomadic tribes, still avoid pork. Nowadays it is usual to give a fabricated medical reason for refusing it, but this is a modern rationalisation for an age-old enmity between the settlers and the nomads.

The pastoral way of life introduced new skills. The shepherd and the goatherd became experts at controlling their flocks. Unlike the settled farmers, they allowed their animals to range more or less freely, feeding themselves, but with some kind of limitation on their wanderings. This was achieved in several ways: for some it meant using dogs or horses to round up the flocks or herds; for others it meant using 'judas animals'. These were specially selected and hand-reared sheep that were trained by the herders to come to them for feeding. With their help they could control the movements of the rest of the flock.

For some shepherds, controlling a large flock became a fine art. Each member of the group had to be known individually and sometimes this led to a spectacular, colourful scene, with brightly marked patches on the back of each animal. Other shepherds scorned this technique, claiming that they could identify each animal as easily as the rest of us can pick out our friends by their faces at a crowded party.

Herding animals involved constant watchfulness, but avoided the drudgery of tilling the fields. It was an attractive contract for both human and animal, stating simply: I will look after you and allow you a full, active and natural life, in exchange for eating you at the end of it.

The contract is still honoured where pastoralists survive in those regions not yet partitioned into neat fields. In Africa, for example, the Masai continue to drive their cattle out to pasture during the day and bring them back to their thorn-ringed enclosures at night, moving to new grounds as the grazing changes. So important to them are their cattle that they are loath to kill them. Instead they take their body fluids – their milk and their blood – and allow the cattle to live on. The animals accept their role as involuntary blood donors with little protest: it seems to be a minor irritation equivalent to a large insect bite. For the grateful Masai there is protein and continued survival. They have resisted all attempts to modify their unsettled way of life which has barely altered over thousands of years. In the simplicity of the contract such pastoralists have with their animals, they are probably the closest reminder we have today of the ancestral hunters.

The cowboys of the American West used to live similar lives, driving their cattle to market after allowing them to graze freely on the wide open plains. Here too the animals looked after themselves with the minimum of interference and control; here too there was less drudgery in the fields but much more surveillance than on the settled, fenced-in farms. Today, however, the situation is very different. Ranching has been replaced by high-tech cattle stations and rearing cattle is now a mechanised, mass-production process. The freedom, for both man and animal, of the old Wild West has become an impersonal conveyor-belt system, to the benefit of neither.

For the humans leading the pleasant pastoral lifestyle, there was, however, one problem: the animals were not actually hunted down. Killing them had become a repetitive, routine matter. What happened to the old hunting urge of mankind, whereby the skills of the human hunters were pitted against dangerous wild animals? Where had the thrills gone, and the tests of stamina and courage? This had become a dilemma even in the earliest civilisations: their response has been revealed to us in the form of dramatic carvings.

The survival hunt became a sport hunt. With the need for hunted food gone, but the urge to enjoy the thrill of the chase remaining, the solution was to hunt for the sake of hunting. The prey was not necessarily eaten: the object of the exercise was to enjoy the risk, the danger, the display of manliness and courage. Any dangerous or elusive animal was at risk, so long as it offered sufficient opposition to provide a challenge.

*   *   *

The Animal Contract had now changed: as primeval hunters we killed only to survive; as sport hunters, with our predatory urges frustrated by increasingly efficient farming techniques, we started to kill for fun. That meant that the range of species attacked widened, and virtually anything that moved became fair game.

In ancient times big-game hunters had already started to write wildly exaggerated accounts of their escapades. They continued the tradition into the early part of the twentieth century. Eventually they had to stop because true-life films revealed them to have been, as one critic dubbed them, 'hairy-Hemingway-cowards'. Before the truth was out, however, they were able to show off outrageously, inventing great ferocity in their prey in order to justify to themselves and to their acquaintances their needless acts of animal slaughter.

Most of the animals that the Victorian big-game hunters shot in India and Africa stood staring dumbly at the raised rifles. To kill them was in reality no more daring than shooting a pet cow on the farm; these new hunters were nothing more than boastful thugs. With their new weapons there was no challenge, but they were driven on by the ancient call of the hunter and had to make their escapades look dangerous and impressive. It was a sad example of a broken contract, between ourselves and some of the world's most graceful and dramatic wildlife.

Today, even though the world has become more sensitive to animal suffering and to the value of studying nature rather than slaughtering it, big-game hunting is still big business. In modern Texas, the affluent can go on home-grown safaris on ranches where exotic game from all over the world is specially bred to be gunned down. Many magnificent game species are available, according to a current price list:

Zebra	$5000
Gazelle	$3000
Oryx	$3000
Bison	$2500
Eland	$2500
Wildebeest	$2000
Blackbuck	$1500
Ibex	$1500
Bobcat	$500
Turkey	$300

They are specially bred on farms and ranches and then released into the Texas countryside for brave hunters to pursue with their telescopic rifles. The colour brochures are full of photographs of grinning clients kneeling by the corpses of their freshly killed animals. The only difference between 1890 and 1990 is that a century ago the big-game hunter placed his foot on the back of his fallen prey when being photographed in triumph; today he merely lifts its head to show off its horns or antlers.

The ranch-breeding of exotic species for hunters in Texas has a long history, beginning in 1930 with the importation of nilgai. Since then 370 ranches have added exotics – or Tex-otics as they are now called – to their stock. A census taken in the 1980s revealed that there were 59 species of exotic game animals being bred and hunted in Texas, and a grand total of 120,201 individual animals. Since they are classed as private property, the animals on these ranches are not protected by the Texas game laws that restrict the open season for local wild game to a brief period each year. Anyone who has the urge to shoot a zebra in the head can do so on any day of the year.

How do the Texan ranchers justify their highly artificial safaris? To many critics this kind of hunting is so contrived that it is acceptable to only the most insensitive. To the ranchers themselves it is a new form of conservation and they defend it vigorously. As one exclaimed recently: 'It's going to be the New Africa. I feel fairly certain that this is something we'll be able to pass on to future generations.'

What they are hoping to pass on are huge herds of wild animals that are flourishing on the Texan grasslands. For the deer, antelope and other exotic imports, the local environment is a paradise and they quickly multiply until their numbers become a positive embarrassment. At present there are over 38,000 axis deer, over 18,000 blackbuck, 15,000 nilgai and 14,000 aoudad. There are more of some species living on the Texan grasslands than in their original homelands. This has produced some strange anomalies. That beautiful Asiatic antelope, the blackbuck, now appears on restaurant menus in parts of Texas, while at the same time the Pakistani government has been forced to go to the great expense of importing fifteen of these animals from Texas to boost their dwindling herds.

If this is the case, what is to stop the Texan ranchers from turning their huge ranches into wildlife game parks, where tourists can come to see and photograph but not shoot the animals? This would enable the ranchers to become true saviours of wildlife, instead of being labelled as bloodthirsty primitives.

Their answer is a simple one of economics. The rich hunters pay so much to spill blood that the income from the safaris makes the conservation schemes possible. As one rancher said, 'We can send endangered species back to their native habitat if they will set us free to raise them. We have got to make some income from somewhere.' If restrictions are placed on the hunting, they insist, the Texotics industry will collapse and all the imported stock will be eliminated. Furthermore, they do not accept the alternative idea of zoo parks as an improvement. Zoo animals, they claim, are soft, pampered things that perish shortly after they have been returned to the wild. The ranch animals, because they are more wary, are more likely to succeed: 'Ranch animals know when to eat different grasses, know a little about predators because there are coyotes and foxes in the area, particularly when they are calving . . . They are more hardy animals, and they are ready to go wild.'

Their final line of defence is that the rich hunters are merely acting as natural predators for the herds, in the absence of such animals as lions, tigers, and wolves. Without them, the herds would quickly overbreed and overpopulate, creating a crisis in food supply. In most herds there is always a surplus of males and it is these that the hunters like to take. Since the hunters prefer to shoot the older males with the biggest horns or antlers, the younger males take over the breeding in a natural way.

As has often been argued in Africa and elsewhere, the limited activities of big-game hunters can be presented as a valuable act of conservation: by means of cropping, they are keeping the balance as nature intended. This argument may enable the conservation-hunters to sleep easy, but it by no means satisfies their opponents. The idealists among their critics refuse even to consider the economics of the situation, insisting that the only aim should be to withdraw our inter-ference with natural populations and leave the balance of nature to take care of itself, as it did long before the human species appeared on the scene. This animal liberation creed demands that we should allow wild animals to live in the wild without disturbing the ancient relations between predators and prey. This is unrealistic, since the damage has already been done, and done on a global scale. The places where the wild is still truly wild are few and far between, and the human population is growing at such a rate that there is no sensible hope of the ideal situation ever returning.

At a less idealistic level, other critics argue that, if any herds are swelling and need to be cropped, this should not be organised on a pleasure basis. The attitude of its killer may not make much difference to a blackbuck, but it does make a considerable difference to the fostering of less aggressive human attitudes towards animals. If surplus animals have to be shot to protect the botanical environment, then this could be done by the ranchers themselves, reluctantly, and as a matter of need. This would avoid keeping alive the bloodlust attitude of the big-game hunters and would gradually rid society of the concept that it is right and proper to take pleasure in spilling animal blood. This concept is already dead and buried for large segments of the population, but the fostering of big-game hunting by the powerful game and gun lobby keeps it very much alive and helps to pass it on to new generations. It is this criticism of the Texotics industry that is valid, but it leaves unanswered the question of the economics of the business. The many thousands of dollars that some individuals are prepared to pay to experience the joy of slaughter must somehow be replaced. The photographic safari is one obvious answer. It may even be possible to create a massive reservoir of wildlife inside the United States that could withstand the onslaught of the human population explosions in the original homelands of the animals concerned.

*   *   *

Today only the very rich can afford the space in which to hunt. The crowded city-dwellers have no such space. This first became a problem in Roman times. The solution was to bring the hunt into the city. To do this, vast amphitheatres were constructed. More than 70 of them were built, the greatest of which was the Colosseum in Rome itself.

For over 400 years the amphitheatres were awash with animal blood. Wild beasts from all over the known world were brought to the Roman cities to be hunted down and

massacred in the huge arenas. On opening day at the Colosseum 5000 animals perished. In the two days that followed,
3000 more were slain. This was hunting run amok. One arena
hunt alone saw the killing of 300 ostriches and 200 alpine
chamois. Nothing was spared. Lions, tigers, bears, bulls,
leopards, giraffe and deer were all slaughtered. Such was the
demand for this debased urban hunting spectacle that the
neighbouring lands were stripped bare of their wildlife. Before
the Roman atrocities began there were elephants in North
Africa, hippopotamuses in Nubia and lions in Mesopotamia.
Before they ended, these had all been exterminated, shipped
out in their thousands and – those that survived the terrible
journeys – slaughtered to the cheers of the city crowds.

The cost of these arena hunts was astronomical, but a
succession of Roman rulers felt they were necessary to keep
the common people amused. An unusually unpopular leader
could curry favour with the Roman populace by staging an
even more spectacular show than his predecessor. It was this
competitive element that led to the worst excesses. Sometimes
this meant impressing by sheer numbers: 500 lions at one
time, or 410 leopards, or 100 bears. Sometimes it required the
introduction of the exotic: hippos, rhinos, or, in one case, 36
crocodiles in a specially built pool. Sometimes it led to new
and ingenious ways of slaughtering the prey, such as decapi-
tating fleeing ostriches with crescent-shaped arrows.

The Roman crowds were always there, cheering on the
bloodshed, but even they found some displays too much to
bear. When 20 adult elephants were pitted against heavily
armed human warriors, the screaming of the giant animals as
they were attacked was so terrible that the crowd booed the
emperor for his cruelty. Nevertheless it was to be a very long
time before the killing was stopped and the animal games

abandoned. Even then, it was probably the mounting expense of the operations rather than their bloodiness that ended them.

From the fifth century onwards, Europe had to be content with more modest forms of urban hunting displays. These became even more debased and cruel, with little courage involved either on the part of the humans or the animals. The most popular forms were bull- and bear-baiting, in which the tethered prey were tormented by dogs. An extract from a handbill advertising such an event in London vividly gives the flavour of these occasions: 'This is to give notice to all gentlemen, gamesters, and others, that on this present Monday is a match to be fought by two dogs . . . at a bull, for a guinea to be spent; likewise a green bull to be baited, which was never baited before; and a bull to be turned loose with fireworks all over him; also a mad ass to be baited, with a variety of bull-baiting and bear-baiting, and a dog to be drawn up with fireworks. Beginning exactly at three of the clock.'

These were shows enjoyed by the common people and royalty alike. Elizabeth I would put on such displays to entertain visiting ambassadors. They were not looked upon as vulgar atrocities, but as normal pastimes to keep people happy. Mayors were even instructed to enforce baiting as one of their official duties. The city of Leicester has an instruction on its record books ordering that 'No butcher shall kill a bull to sell within the town before it is baited.' Not until the seventeenth century do we find voices raised against this urban hunting sport. Samuel Pepys wrote in his diary that he had taken his wife to see bulls attacked by dogs, 'but it is a very rude and nasty pleasure'. A few years later, John Evelyn wrote in his diary that, after attending with friends some bull- and bear-baiting, he was 'most heartily weary of the rude and dirty pastime'.

Despite these important voices being raised against it, the urban slaughter was to continue into the nineteenth century, until it was outlawed by an Act of Parliament in 1835. Opponents of the Act argued that the abolition of animal-baiting would 'lead to a softening of the national character, which would cause Britain to lose her high place in the world', but the Act went through despite these protests. Gradually, across the globe, arena blood sports began to disappear.

It is hard to understand the pleasure people took in the torture and slaughter of trapped animals, but there is a modern reminder of it. The pathetically operatic bullfight, the last remnant of that earlier, barbaric age, is still disgracing our civilisation.

The survival of bull-killing when the other forms of urban display-slaughter have been ostracised requires some explanation. The great, charging bull has always been seen as the epitome of brute strength and virile animal power. For a man to slay such a fearsome beast was such a mark of heroism that the act became endowed with religious significance from very early days. In a way it became the supreme ceremonial embodiment of man's primeval hunting courage. Bull-cults spread all over the ancient world and were one of the main rivals to Christianity. Remnants of this concept of the ritual slaughter of the great beast survived to medieval times, when brave knights would display their skill by lancing a bull from horseback. This practice was outlawed by the Pope in the sixteenth century, not because it was a cruel spectacle in which horses were often disembowelled and bulls were slow to die, but because too many fine noblemen were being seriously injured. Such was the papal priority. The edict had little effect, but eventually in the eighteenth century so many useful cavaliers were being killed by bulls that it was finally forbidden to the aristocracy.

Their role was taken over by the slaughterhousemen of Seville. Having no horses, they fought on foot, making a much more daring spectacle, and the matador was born. He soon found that he could earn far more money slaughtering his bulls in a public arena than in the privacy of the slaughterhouse. Tired old horses were brought into the ring to be gored by the bulls as an entertaining preliminary. The fact that the thousands of spectators relished these bloodlettings is one of the more worrying aspects of the human personality. For most of us the hunting urge can easily be transformed into some symbolic equivalent, but the ease with which it can revert to its primeval form is startling. The bullfight is not a rare event but a major sport, with 450 bullrings worldwide. The majority are in Spain but there are over 80 in Mexico, and others in Venezuela, Peru, Colombia, Ecuador and Bolivia, as well as a few in southern France. For some reason, it seems to be a strictly Catholic sport, despite the papal edict. Portugal also has bullrings, but there the bull is spared the climax of its torment and is not killed in the ring. (It is, however, slaughtered soon afterwards.)

In Spain alone there are at least 1000 bullfights annually, with about 4500 bulls dying. Each bull takes about 15 minutes to meet its end. While the spectacle is in progress it has been a traditional custom to cook the testicles of the first bull killed and serve them to the dignitaries present while they watch the later bulls die. This tells us something about the true nature of the bullfight: the bull is not seen as a bull but as a primordial symbol. It is the symbol that is being overpowered, not a suffering animal that is being tortured to death.

It can be argued that the contract is not as harsh as it might appear. The bull is allowed to live for four or five years, twice as long as the typical beef bull, and spends those years in the lap of bovine luxury. He has no foreknowledge of what is to befall him and, once in the ring, his adrenalin is flowing so fast that, like a soldier in battle, he can hardly feel the injuries that are inflicted upon him. The death is no worse than that experienced by a buffalo being torn to pieces by a pack of wild dogs.

That is the defence of the bullfight, but it is hard for the objective observer to enjoy the expressions on the faces of the spectators. The bull may suffer slightly less than critics claim, but can the minds behind the faces of the excited audience really take more pleasure in seeing the magnificent animal die rather than live? If they can so distance themselves from living things, then they have swallowed the dangerous fairy tale that places mankind above nature. If the bull is a symbol of nature, we are re-enacting its ritual destruction and gloating over its fall. What this means for the future of our biosphere is alarming, to say the least.

For those who listen for them, the alarm bells could be heard ringing again, if only faintly, in the southern states of America in the 1960s and again in the 1980s. In Louisiana it was seriously suggested that arena blood sports of the Roman kind should once again be staged for public entertainment. In 1969 it was proposed that contests between men and lions should be presented, employing state athletic facilities, for a paying audience. The lion-fighting would be conducted 'on a special surface that would be disadvantageous to the animal'. It would be a composition surface that would prevent the lion from getting a grip with its claws. This would make it skid and slip, to make the contest more even and give the human opponent a chance to run the lion through with his sword. The proposers of the idea were quick to point out that the use of a sand arena by the ancient Romans had been a grave error:

'Any history book tells you that the Christians tried to go against the lions in sand and the fights didn't last long enough for the crowd to get settled.' Clearly this would be bad for the popcorn sales.

The revival of the idea in 1988, following its rejection in the 1960s, was due to the publicity about the lion-hunts in neighbouring Texas, where pet lions had been let loose on a 50-acre island to be gunned down for a price of $3500 per animal. If Texas could stage that kind of event, then what was wrong with lion-fighting in which the humans involved were armed with nothing more than a sword? Surely this was more courageous and more acceptable? Even though, according to its proposers, 'the tax receipts from lion-fighting are needed by the state treasury', it is doubtful whether this new tourist attraction would have caught on. During the fifteen centuries since it was last staged there have been new alternatives on offer that provide strong competition.

Happily, most people today find arena blood sports repulsive rather than enjoyable. We may have evolved as hunters preying on large animals, but times have changed. We no longer need to pursue animal prey, and most of the gruesome alternatives involving animals are no longer acceptable. The various blood sports have gradually been replaced in the public's affections by a more abstract contest, the arena ball sport. Football has taken the place of animal slaughter.

*　　*　　*

Modern ball sports are now the most popular tribal gatherings known to our species. Every week millions of people gather to watch their tribal heroes attempt to score goals, or win some other kind of sporting competition. The hunt is on, but not for animals. There are still targets, but when the modern sportsman hits the bull's-eye, no bull dies. Everything about sport is derived from the hunt: there is no sport in existence that does not base itself either on the chase or on aiming, the two key elements of primeval hunting.

There are those who see sports as symbolic forms of warfare. Although there is an element of truth in this interpretation, their deeper significance is in the way they offer the modern citizen a re-creation of the ancient tribesman's prey-killing sequence. We were, after all, hunting for a million years before we went to war. At the root of war there is always a territorial dispute and in our earliest days we must have been far too scarce to have suffered many territorial clashes. On the other hand, we did experience regular pangs of hunger that set us off on hunt after hunt, day after day, moulding our species into its new personality. It is that personality that finds expression in today's bloodless sports. The hunting field that was replaced by the ancient arena has now become the modern stadium.

All the features of the primeval hunt are present in a typical team game: the group co-operation, the planning and preparation, the specialised equipment, the strategies and tactics, the tribal colours and emblems, the risks and physical dangers, the bravery and cunning, the accidents and injuries, the tricks and traps, and, above all, the vigorous chase and the deadly aim. But when the target is found, no animal bleeds, for the quarry is pursued by the symbolic hunters of the twentieth century.

In these sports there is no cruelty to animals, for there are no animals to kill. What happens to human bodies during violent sporting encounters is often far from benign, but at least the tribesmen have volunteered for this damaging way of life and, despite the injuries, it carries many basic rewards: the harsh physical nature of the events is something to which the human body is well attuned. We evolved to be physically active, and those of us who pass our adult lives sitting behind a desk risk far worse damage to our bodies through abnormal levels of physical inactivity. The tribal sportsman is closer to nature than we are. Proof of this is found in the gentle nature of many of these men away from the stadium: it is we, the urban desk-dwellers, who are left simmering with aggression after a day's work. They are physically fulfilled: as modern hunters they can relax, because they have nothing to prove.

A football match is not a casual pastime but a desperately serious business. Unable to hunt for themselves, twentieth-century tribesmen must find expression for their primeval urges in this substitute activity. As each game begins, the watching eyes observe the re-enactment of a ritual hunt. The goalmouth is the prey and it must be killed with the new tribal weapon: the ball. The furore caused by the scoring of a goal is out of all proportion to the superficial nature of the act – the passing of a curved piece of leather between two uprights – but its deeper, symbolic meaning is powerful enough to make normally quiet, reticent men leap and shout and roar themselves hoarse with excitement. Nowhere else in modern society do we see such extreme expression of elation and depression, of triumph and despair.

It is no accident that football is by far the most popular sport worldwide, with its organising body, FIFA, flying more flags than even the United Nations. It contains more elements of the primeval hunt sequence than any other type of sporting contest. Like the hunt it is a highly unpredictable event. It is always hard to guess where the action will move next, where the ball will fly, and who will have it. The players are seen to demonstrate both speed and agility on the one hand, and stamina and concentration on the other. The long, free-flowing game requires both physical strength and a cool head. The rules are simple and easy to understand and the action is played out just as if the watchers are witnessing a human hunting pack bearing down on their prey. Goals are rare, averaging only one per game for each team. This makes them special in the way that bringing down a difficult prey animal was special.

The weakness of this symbolic hunt is that the prey, the goalmouth, is static. This is necessary to keep the game within the arena for the watching tribal followers, but it makes the prey too easy to hit. To correct this there is the opposing team, with its goalkeeper, defending the goalmouth and making it into a challenge worthy of the prowess of the brave hunters. The opposing team has often been called the enemy, as though this is a battle between two armies, but it is nothing of the kind. The other players are there to make the goal-scoring more difficult for our pack of goal-hunters. Indeed, if they are actually treated as the enemy and attacked, the referee immediately intervenes and punishes those hunters who have, momentarily, become warriors.

Many other sports offer almost as much of the hunting sequence as soccer and also enjoy considerable support. The other styles of football – Canadian, American, Australian, Gaelic and Rugby – as well as hockey, ice hockey, polo, water polo, cricket, baseball, lacrosse, basketball and the lesser-known team games all involve the tactics, the chasing and the aiming of a missile at a goal of some kind. There are the sports that stress the aiming element almost to the exclusion of everything else: archery, darts, shooting, javelin, billiards, snooker, pool, bowling, boules, curling, golf, jai alai, squash, tennis, badminton and table tennis. Each of these tests the pseudo-hunter's skill at being precisely on target. In a different category are the sports that concentrate solely on that other key element of the hunt: the chase. Sports chasing takes the form of racing, with a vehicle of some kind, a steed, or unassisted. Included here are such ancient sports as track athletics, along with more modern pursuits such as orienteering.

When they are classified in this way, it soon becomes clear that all modern sports are derived from key elements in the primeval hunt and now represent a major, if unconscious, outlet for the frustrated hunting drive of the modern urban tribesman. If this were not so it is highly likely that all these physical activities would remain at the schoolboy-play level and never be taken seriously by adults. Bearing in mind that they now take up almost as much space in the newspapers as topics such as politics and finance, it is clear that they have a much more powerful significance in society than the mere act of 'hitting a ball about' would seem to justify. Long may it be so, for sport is not only harmless to animals, but diverts millions of followers from possible alternatives that could all too easily contain elements of animal persecution.

*   *   *

Our hunting urges may be sublimated in sport, but what has happened to that other ancient technique for providing us with food? With the hunting taken out of it, what has befallen the world of farming?

Some farm animals are well cared for and given the space in

108

which to fulfil their natural urges and perform their behavioural activities. They live in large, splendid, open-range farms. The majority, however, are not so lucky. They have become the inmates of animal concentration camps called intensive farms. In reality these are not farms at all. They are factories in which domestic livestock are treated like machinery. The factory owners are not farmers, but ruthless businessmen. All is not well down on the farm in the late twentieth century.

In its never-ending search for increased economy and increased production to feed the 5000 million naked apes on earth at present, farming has sunk almost as low as it is possible to get in terms of Animal Contracts. The jolly farmer with a farmyard full of hens and ducks and geese, and a few pigs nosing in a nearby field, is already an antique. We still print pictures of him in our children's books, but in reality he is a rare and vanishing species. In his place are businessmen and accountants. They make simple calculations: how little space can they give each animal without killing it? How little comfort does it need before it will go into a decline and fail to meet its quota? How much environmental deprivation can it be made to undergo before its condition will suffer and reduce the company's profits? These are the only considerations that enter their minds when designing their long, bleak, anonymous buildings that disfigure our countryside.

In Britain 400,000 sows are kept shut up in tiny stalls only two feet wide, standing or lying for most of their lives on cold concrete. Twenty-nine million turkeys are fattened each year in windowless sheds. What is being done to veal calves is hard to credit. It is a particularly bad time to be a farm animal, especially if you happen to be a chicken.

In most countries the vast majority of hens are kept in

intensive batteries. In Britain 96 per cent of all egg-laying hens are kept in factory farms. There are 40 million of them, usually housed five to a cage measuring no more than 18 × 20 inches. That gives each hen a living space with an area less than that of a sheet of typing paper. They spend their entire adult lives in these cages. At birth they are separated into males and females. The male chicks are immediately killed by gassing. At 18 weeks of age the hens are placed in their tiny cages where they must stand on the sloping wire floors laying their eggs until, at about 70 weeks of age, they are slaughtered.

Each hen gives us about 300 eggs. In exchange we give it the most deprived life we can devise without actually stopping it laying: it is another broken contract. Little wonder that many of the birds become aggressive and have to be de-beaked. Official advice about using beak-trimming machines has been given to the farmers: 'An upper blade has a sharp edge, is electrically heated and closes onto an unheated lower blade. A portion of the beak is thus removed and the stump cauterised in one operation. In young chicks the cutting edge is not used – the desired effect is achieved by pressing the tip firmly against the heated blade. Great care is needed with young birds not to damage the tongue or nostrils.' It does not seem to occur to the authors of this advisory leaflet that, if it is necessary to remove something as basic to a bird as part of its beak, then there must be something fundamentally wrong with the agricultural system that is in operation. They do not even have the excuse that a free-range system of hen-keeping is impossible: it is merely more expensive, adding a few extra pennies to the price of each box of eggs in the supermarket.

The factory farmers, needless to say, blame the housewife, insisting that she will not buy the more expensive eggs, but they make sure that she is as unaware as possible of the living conditions of the hens whose eggs she does buy. Battery-produced eggs are deliberately advertised as 'farm fresh eggs' with slogans such as 'a taste of the country' accompanied by pretty paintings of fields and trees. The busy housewife can hardly be blamed for grabbing a box of eggs that is slightly cheaper from the supermarket shelves. Those to blame are the businessmen who profit directly from extreme environmental deprivation of domestic animals.

The Animal Contract has been reduced to nothing more than callous exploitation. The more an animal species has had to offer us, with its flesh or its produce, the worse has been its lot. Instead of honouring the animals that serve us so well, we have degraded them to the level of animal machines. How can we have allowed this to happen at a time when we have in so many other ways become so sensitive to suffering and so vociferous in our condemnation of the infliction of unnecessary pain?

Originally, farming was a response to human population growth, but it became a cause of it. In the first 3000 years of farming the human population exploded from 2–3 million to 100 million. As populations rose and farms grew in size, intimacy with animals began to be lost. Space was at a premium and new techniques were introduced to cope. Gradually the process became more impersonal and cost-effective. After the Second World War the idea of intensive farming was introduced and flourished. Now, in a factory farm, it became possible for one man to service 20,000 hens.

Farm animals have become nothing more than meat on legs. Converted into food, they are neatly packaged with all signs of nature removed. City children were asked, in a survey, to say where eggs came from. From the supermarket, they replied. But where did they come from before that? They shrugged.

The reason why so many people are prepared to eat food produced in a factory farm is that their human lives are so remote from it: by the time they see the food it is wrapped in clingfilm on a supermarket shelf. They sometimes seem to forget that it doesn't start out like that.

It is easy to understand how sensitive people begin to have second thoughts about their diets when they find out about factory farms or slaughterhouses. According to recent market research, about one in twenty of the British population is a vegetarian or vegan and the numbers are on the increase. Several motives are involved. For some individuals it is a matter of religious belief, often connected with Buddhist doctrines. For others it is part of a philosophy that requires self-denial: a survey investigating the vegetarian personality revealed that the majority are against vaccination, blood transfusion, immunisation, contraception, smoking and drinking. For many others the reason for giving up meat is simply to avoid being an accessory to the killing of an animal.

Interestingly, the survey showed that the majority of vegetarians are also opposed to pet-keeping and, since the vast majority of pets are cats and dogs, this means that they are not even prepared to be accessories to animal-killing at second hand. Since cats and dogs are carnivores, to feed them would mean buying meat for them and this too is unacceptable, even though the meat is not for their own human consumption. This has led some vegetarians, who wish to keep pet cats and dogs, to impose a vegetarian diet on their animal companions. It has to be said that, with cats in particular, this is an extreme cruelty and the vegetarian societies issuing leaflets recommending vegetarian diets for cats – diets that will certainly cause them a painful death – are vulnerable to accusations of cruelty to animals.

The dilemma of the pet cat highlights the difficulty of the vegetarian's position. The world is made up of carnivores and herbivores, predators and prey. An objective observer of animal life cannot take sides in their relationship. Without the carnivores, the herbivores would overbreed and desolate their landscape. Without the herbivores the carnivores would starve to death. Together they make up the balance of nature. To interfere with this balance is an emotional folly. We must respect the carnivore's way of life as much as the herbivore's. In the same way we must respect the right of our pet cats and dogs to exist.

Equally, we humans, as evolved carnivores, have the right to live by our natural diet. Mankind is irreversibly adapted to a diet that contains meat as a major constituent and is no longer suited to a predominantly vegetable diet. Proof of this comes from those struggling peasant populations where meat is in short supply. Populations forced to suffer a low-protein, high-carbohydrate diet for prolonged periods eventually succumb to cirrhosis of the liver, pellagra, beriberi, kwashiorkor and other serious deficiency diseases.

George Bernard Shaw, one of history's most famous vegetarians, is often cited as an example of a man who lived actively into his nineties through his special diet, but the truth is that he survived despite it, not because of it. Serious anaemia, caused by his vegetarianism, was threatening to kill him at one stage and he could only be saved by accepting medication that included liver extracts. This made the leaders of the vegetarian movement furious and they savagely attacked the elderly playwright, apparently caring more for principles than for Shaw's continued survival. Shaw wrote a withering reply, in which he made the crucial point that the value of vegetarianism is greatly diminished by the fact that it is so difficult and expensive to do well, ending with the comment: 'The so-called simple life is beyond the means of the poor.'

For those who have not studied the problem this may be difficult to understand. Vegetables are cheaper than meat but the problem is one of balancing the intake of vegetables in order to produce, by human cunning, the amino-acid balance so simply offered by every piece of meat. Different vegetables possess different essential amino acids, but not in the right combination: without the perfect combination of all eight of them, none of them works properly in the human digestive system. This means that, to produce a safe vegetarian meal, a delicate balance based on biochemical knowledge has to be achieved, employing just the right mixture of botanical elements. This requires patience and expertise and explains why it is that, in ignorant peasant communities, the unavoidable vegetable diet causes so many serious deficiency diseases. As things are at present, an efficient vegetarian diet is essentially a phenomenon of the affluent middle classes. By contrast, a crudely applied vegetarian diet for the masses remains a killer.

Vegetarians are quick to point out that this need not always be so: if advanced nutritional knowledge were applied on a global scale, so that a carefully balanced plant diet could be mass-produced in starvation areas, there is hope that the terrible deficiencies caused by the absence of sufficient meat could be avoided. This is clearly a prospect for the future and an important one, since it seems that in any case there will never be enough meat for everyone.

There are additional difficulties, however, because certain crucial vitamins and minerals are missing from a purely botanical diet, even the most expertly balanced one. Clearly, the vegetarian movement, despite its good intentions, is fighting against nature, and its unequal struggle will continue until that far-off day when our biochemists have eventually succeeded in creating a complete synthetic diet from basic chemicals for us all to eat.

If meat is necessary for nutritional reasons, it must be admitted that its consumption makes hypocrites of many of us. Modern citizens love their joints of meat and their steaks, but how many of them would be prepared to carry out the killing, the degutting and the butchering themselves? Isolation from farming and from hunting has made us squeamish. We live in an age of specialisation, when matters of life and death are kept discreetly at a distance. If we had to do the killing, many more of us would resort to the vegetarian or vegan solution than do so already. Those who market our food are well aware of this, which is why so much meat today is displayed in shapeless cellophane packets which give no hint of its natural animal origins. It is abstract food for a generation that prefers not to associate the meat it eats with the animals from which it comes.

There is nothing shameful about killing animals solely as a source of food. What is shameful, however, is the manner in which we treat many of them before we kill them. We all have to die, both humans and non-humans, but neither we nor they need to live miserable lives. There is no excuse for inflicting pain, frustration or deprivation on any of our food animals at any stage in their lives. Death may be inevitable but cruelty is not. If we must eat meat, then we must ensure that the animals we kill for our food live the best possible lives before they die. Anything less is a betrayal of the Animal Contract.

*   *   *

Meat is not the only thing we take from animals. For centuries we have trapped them for their fur. When fur-trapping began there was some excuse for it. As human cultures spread to increasingly remote and hostile corners of the world, the peoples facing these harsh new terrains were struggling for survival. The Inuit in the far north, for example, would have frozen to death without taking the winter coats of other species long adapted to the frozen wastelands. Furs, to the Inuit, were a barrier between their naked human bodies and a certain icy death: but they killed only in order to live, and only for themselves. When the fur-trappers moved in, they were motivated by greed; their disregard for the animals they trapped was entirely callous. A nightmare for fur-bearing animals was about to begin, and countless millions of them would perish in pain and misery. The age of the spring-trap, with its brutal metal jaws, was upon us.

These traps catch the animals and hold their legs for several hours before they can be approached, terrified, by trappers and bludgeoned or choked to death in a way that will not spoil the quality of their pelts. A quick death by shooting to replace the long suffering of the traps is out of the question because of the holes it makes in the precious skins. It is an agonising death and its only purpose is to provide us with a type of clothing we do not need.

Spring-traps have already been outlawed in 66 countries, because of attention focused on the extreme cruelty involved, but three major countries have held out against the ban and retain this brutal technique which shames their inhabitants. Those countries are the Soviet Union, Canada and the United States. Needless to say, these are also the major fur-trading countries, so that the trapping continues on a grand scale, despite the voices raised against it in so many regions.

Millions of animals die in the steel-jawed leg-traps of those three countries every year. This is not just a matter of another broken leg, but of yet another broken contract. It is difficult to obtain accurate figures, but the estimated total number of wild animals caught in traps annually in the 1980s is 20 million. This huge figure is by no means unusual for the fur trade. In earlier decades, when the fashion for wearing exotic furs was at its height, it was even greater. A century ago, for example, we know that 9,852,000 furs passed through London alone. Multiply this by all the other major cities dealing in furs and the enormity of the operation begins to sink in.

Just as the housewife buying factory-farmed food is not callous, so the woman slipping into her mink coat is not cruel, but merely sheltered from another animal truth. She saw the beauty of the fur and could not resist it. What she did not see at close quarters was the cost in animal suffering. What protects her is the remoteness of the trapping grounds, far away in the cold forests of the northern hemisphere: out of sight and therefore out of mind. They promise to stay that way unless public opinion can be swayed by exposure to the harsh truth behind the trappings.

The defence put forward by the fur-trappers, when challenged about the ethics of their trade, is predictable. They claim to be helping the conservation movement. Conservationists, they point out, have to crop species that become too abundant and this is the principle on which they, too, are operating. They are protecting the fur-bearing species. As one of them put it: 'If fur coats are not bought and worn, the animals from which we harvest the fur would become extinct through disease and starvation caused by overpopulation. The fur trade are the true friends of the earth and conservation of wildlife is our watchword.' By trapping millions of animals every year they are keeping the numbers down to an efficient level. The conservation movement will no doubt be alarmed to discover what strange bedfellows they have acquired as a result of their official cropping policies. What are the true facts in the case of the fur trade? Is there any validity in their argument? It is much the same as the one used by the fox-hunting world.

The short answer is that the carnivorous fur-bearing animals – the foxes, wolves, otters, mink, sable, raccoons, cats and bears – all have their own built-in population-control mechanisms. If they suffer from slight overcrowding they quickly reduce their level of breeding. They do this by a variety of means, including reduced ovulation by females, reduced mating, failure to conceive, spontaneous abortion, re-absorption of the embryos, or failure to rear the young. For non-predatory species the natural level of predation often does play a part and if their normal predators are exterminated by mankind, then the prey species may, in certain instances, overpopulate. The answer in such instances, of course, is to leave the natural predators to deal with the situation.

There is therefore little or no justification for man to trap the fur-bearing species in the wild. The best and only acceptable form of conservation is to leave the prey and predators to relate to one another naturally, as they had done for millions of years before mankind came on to the scene. This is not always possible today in areas of high human population, but in the frozen north, where so many of the wild fur-bearers live, it is still a feasible proposition and should, in any case, always remain the ultimate ideal.

In the 1920s certain fur traders themselves became sickened by the barbarity of the trapping method and suggested a reform. They proposed the development of fur farms where fur-bearing animals could be bred in cages like domestic animals. They pleaded that, 'If for no other than humane reasons, fur ranching should be looked upon favorably, and encouraged by every one having an appreciable idea of the untold agony and frightful torture which fur-bearing animals must undergo if we may obtain them from the wilds.' It is pleasant to think of them showing so much concern, but there may have been a simpler explanation. Elsewhere, more honestly perhaps, the same authority commented: 'the natural source of our fur supply is rapidly vanishing; consequently, the necessity of fur raising is being forced upon us to offset a further shortage in our annual fur crop from the wilds'.

Whatever the true motive, fur-raising and fur-ranching gradually grew in importance. Currently 35 million mink are produced from fur farms worldwide each year. In theory, the farming of mink provides a reasonably good Animal Contract, and a senior official of the Humane Society of America was even prepared to write, 'Mink and chinchilla adapt well and are akin to farmed animals such as sheep . . . If you wear mink or chinchilla, you might perhaps come into my home, but don't even think twice about buying a natural, wild animal fur.' In practice, however, the contract is not so attractive. Mink farms have rapidly become mink factories. Intensive farming practices have struck again.

In the wild, the mink, a solitary territorial carnivore with an immensely high activity level, lives on home ranges that may be nearly four miles long. On the fur farms, the mink is given a small wire cage that is at most two and a half feet long. Recommended sizes are $18 \times 18 \times 18$ inches, or $24 \times 15 \times 12$ inches, or $30 \times 9 \times 15$ inches. Normally two mink are placed in each of these tiny containers, where they remain for the whole of their lives. In some states in America cages have been reduced to as little as 6 inches in width to keep more animals in a given space.

The result of this degree of confinement is that the animals exhibit all the typical reactions of wild creatures to a restricted and deprived environment. They perform stereotyped patterns of movement and various forms of self-mutilation. These are clear signs to any objective observer that the captive animals are under stress. Bearing in mind the fact that the size of their natural living space in the wild is approximately 12,000 times as great as their captive living space, this is not entirely surprising. The only way that animals such as mink could be kept in captivity without totally distorting their lifestyles would be to house them in large enclosures where they had plenty of space to exercise and move about. It will never be a practical proposition to provide them with enclosures of this size. Economically it does not make sense and will therefore never happen. An alternative that does not seem to occur to the fur trade is that it might be simpler for people to find other forms of warm clothing. If guns spoil the pelts, traps cause acute pain, and incarceration in tiny cages causes prolonged chronic pain, there is no other solution.

Fur is not the only form of animal coat that we have attempted to transfer from its proper place on to our own bodies. Brightly coloured feathers have for thousands of years also held a special fascination for human eyes where body adornment is concerned. Few tribal societies have failed to add at least a few ornamental plumes to their ritual displays and the craze for feathered accessories has occasionally reached outlandish proportions. Throughout the nineteenth century, ladies of fashion everywhere were determined to outdo one another with their avian apparel. The trade in exotic bird feathers became a major international business. In the fashion centre of Paris there were no fewer than 10,000 people employed exclusively in this bizarre feather industry.

The exquisite plumes of the egret were amongst the most favoured of bird decorations. One South American country alone managed to slaughter 1½ million egrets in a single year to supply the European market. To give some idea of the demand, a single lot at a London auction was for the feathers from 24,000 egrets. The hunters who collected the feathers preferred to shoot parent birds tending their nests, because at that time they were less likely to flee and this made the slaughter easier. As a result of the wiping out of whole colonies of adults, all the nestlings died of starvation, thus adding to the extermination of the birds from whole regions of the world.

Ostrich plumes were also popular and in 1838 the first ostrich farm was established in South Africa. By 1840 more than 1000 kilos of feathers were being exported annually and this figure rose until by 1910 it had reached 370,000 kilos a year. Many other species – the beautiful birds of paradise, parrots, finches, buntings, hawks and pheasants – were all attacked for their exotic plumage, which found its way on to the ornate hats of otherwise kindly and fastidious ladies. The records are astonishing: 300,000 albatrosses from a single Pacific island in one collection, 32,000 humming birds in a single purchase by a leading feather dealer in London. The whims of the fashion world have a lot to answer for.

It was specifically this trade in exotic plumage that led to the formation, at the end of the last century, of the various bird protection societies, both in Europe and North America. It took them several decades to end the female obsession with feathered trimmings, but eventually they managed it in the early part of the twentieth century. Ladies of fashion returning from Europe were startled to discover that New York customs officers were taking the new laws seriously. To their great distress they were forced to moult their feathers at the customs barrier – with a little help from official scissors. Europe was soon to follow suit. After importing 300 million dead birds each year at the height of the fashion, there was suddenly a different atmosphere in the Roaring Twenties, and the wild birds of the world could fly a little more safely at last.

Generally speaking, birds are loved but reptiles are feared. The use of the beautiful skins of giant snakes, lizards and crocodiles has not been so easy to eradicate. The fashion for reptile-skin handbags, shoes and boots – even the occasional snakeskin jacket – has survived in many areas right up to the present time and there is a booming business in crocodile-farming. Hundreds of thousands of these fascinating but greatly reviled animals are slaughtered annually. Many are skinned alive, their reptilian nature arousing few feelings of sympathy or pity in their captors or in those who never pause to wonder at their amazing qualities or marvel at their unique biological features.

We have no essential need for these skins. They are luxury items. Crocodiles, rapidly disappearing all over the world, need them far more than we do. Everywhere we are stripping the wilds of their surviving animals. The crocodiles are literally stripped of their skins to make expensive handbags, elephants are robbed of their ivory tusks and rhinos of their horns, all for no good purpose whatever.

Not content with pillaging the forests for furs, feathers and scales, we also plundered the oceans for blubber. This too was an animal's outer covering, its protection against the cold, but this time we did not wear it: instead we processed it into oil. In the present century alone, the human species has managed to harpoon, kill and dismember more than 1½ million whales, reducing the world population to a fraction of its numbers before our violent technology invaded its peaceful domain. From different parts of the whale's body we have been able to manufacture cosmetics, lubricants, pet food, fertiliser and margarine, as well as using the meat itself, and strips of whalebone for corsets and umbrellas. The scale of the operation has, like the gentle whales themselves, been gigantic. Of the biggest species of all – the vast Blue Whale – we have destroyed 486,000 of the world population of 500,000. The whales are being blown to extinction with explosive harpoons by greedy nations with little understanding of the planetary crime they are committing. The protesters do their best but the vessels of commerce outweigh them all too easily. Only a massive shift in public attitudes can save the leviathans now, but all too often, where conscience should rule, there is only apathy, and the whale populations sink lower and lower. They will soon be gone and the world will be poorer for their loss. They lead complex, sensitive lives, full of mysteries, with their deep booming song, always varying, sending messages to one another across huge expanses of water. Yet another remarkable animal is exploited and belittled by man's dominion over the wild beasts.

*　　*　　*

The catalogue of our folly is depressing. The surface has only been scratched here. Deliberately omitted are the extreme horrors and the unspeakable cruelties. If all the evidence was included – the torments suffered in the name of science by

123

experimental animals in laboratories, the savageries meted out to pet animals by vandals, the bloody pleasures of animal fight organisers, and the rest – then, if you cared enough, you would simply have to stop reading this book. That would be self-defeating. This is one of the great dilemmas of this topic of man–animal relations: to delve into the subject fully is to encounter aspects of human nature so appalling that anyone wishing to do something about it cannot face the facts, and turns away in disgust. Only a few brave spirits are prepared to grasp the nettle and they are frequently rewarded by being labelled as cranks. In this way the great bulk of the population can keep a discreet distance from the unpalatable and smother their guilt with intense preoccupations elsewhere.

How can all this have happened in this modern enlightened age? Are we really such monsters? What has caused us to break so many of our Animal Contracts? It is not enough to say that a policy of remoteness can allow us to become callous without our meaning to be so. There has to be another, additional factor at work.

The answer, yet again, is overpopulation. Quite simply, the human species has become too successful. We have overbred ourselves to the point where we are not only losing touch with our animal background, but are also becoming chronically stressed. The stress caused by overcrowding is a well-known phenomenon in the animal world. It happens to lemmings when they suffer a population explosion. In a lemming year they seem to lose their senses, become hyperactive and start rushing around in all directions. They become aggressive, frenzied and then die of various stress diseases. We are heading this way as a species. In far too many countries populations are doubling with every generation. It is only a matter of time before we hit the human equivalent of a lemming year.

On our way to this state our increasing stress makes us increasingly tense and hostile. We express this largely through redirected aggression, starting from the top of society and working down, with small insults growing into larger social savageries. Finally, at the bottom of the social order are the animals: they cannot answer us back and they cannot report the names of their tormentors. Cases of animal cruelty are soaring in even the most affluent countries. Brutality and indifference abound. Somehow we manage to ignore it without feeling too uncomfortable.

Animal welfare organisations struggle to help as best they can, but it is a daunting task. The pressures of modern life breed cruelty, and the increasing remoteness of nature breeds indifference. Happily, concern for the biosphere is beginning to mount and more voices are being raised in protest about the way we have treated the natural world, but it is not enough to assuage our feelings by being kind to nice animals. Pandas and other attractive rare species are important, but an animal should not have to be rare in order to warrant our sympathy. It is a sad irony that the more successful an animal is and the greater its generosity towards us, the less well we treat it.

Science is making its own attempts to improve the situation. Genetic engineering, much feared by some, is being employed to create new breeds of livestock. Startling new laboratory techniques permitting embryo storage and transfer, gene-splicing and transfer, cloning and multiple ovulation will all enable farmers to develop greatly improved livestock: farm animals capable of resisting disease, living in different environments, producing more milk or meat, and possessing more docile temperaments. Already, sheep have been produced in the laboratory by cloning: the animals are identical in every respect, and even have identical rates of growth. They can be seen as freaks of nature which should be outlawed, or, more positively, as fascinating novelties to be cherished and developed, for the possibilities offered by the brave new world of this 'new agriculture' are enormous. It will mean much greater efficiency on the farm to the extent that farmers will need far less land to create the same amount of produce: millions of acres of farmland will be released from its present inefficient usage by the new biotechnical revolution.

That is the theory, but in practice the danger is that these new trends could lead to even more intensive factory farming, with farm animals designed, as it were, to fit straight into the supermarket tray.

Organic farmers are deeply sceptical about the agricultural uses of genetic engineering. They argue that it merely replaces the environmental manipulation of the factory farmers with genetic manipulation that abuses farm animals in a new way. For the organic farmers, matters have already gone too far down the technical scientific road. They believe that further so-called improvements will only exploit farm animals even more, and that the typical modern dairy cow is already being pushed to limits that cause stress. Under intense pressure to produce the maximum yield of milk, her health often suffers; once she is past her peak period of production, at about five years, she is killed and replaced. By contrast, cattle reared using organic farming methods in fields free from pesticides and chemicals enjoy a lifespan more than twice as long. They may produce less milk, but it is considered to be of a much higher quality. Many consumers are beginning to demand this type of produce, even if it does cost slightly more.

The time has come when we must accept that it is wrong to

apply the harsher rules of commerce to the lives of animals. We must accept that quality of life is as important for them as it is for us. The argument that a particular way of treating animals is profitable is not appropriate, although it is often applied.

Animals are living beings, just like us: they suffer like us and seek comfort like us. We understand them too well now to be able to treat them brutally, as we once did. We must find new ways of fulfilling our side of our contracts with them. If we must kill them, for food or for some other aspect of essential human survival, then we must ensure that they live the best lives we can give them before they die. This is something that should be on our minds every time we buy a piece of meat or crack open an egg.

The problem we face is how to feed the teeming millions of humans that will double their numbers in a few generations. A century from now there simply will not be enough of our planet left to house both us and our domestic animals. In a few hundred years there will not even be room for the crops that satisfy the vegans and vegetarians. What is the solution if we cannot suppress our uncontrolled desire to overpopulate the globe? There is only one and that has little appeal. It is to start research now to develop artificial foods: synthetic, chemically produced meat and vegetables. We must learn to make it taste like real food, to look like it and smell like it in order to tempt our palates. There is no other hope for our species unless we can learn to curb our procreative urges. What will happen to farm animals then is hard to say. Perhaps a few of them will live on as animated museum pieces, to remind us of the early days when farming was still a viable proposition. Perhaps they will disappear altogether, their phase of usefulness over, their time past. In their going, we should look back on them with gratitude and with warmth. They nourished us for 10,000 years, shared life and death with us, and always gave us more than we gave them. Without them, civilisation itself would have been impossible.

III

Man's Best Friends

Man's Best Friends

The human species is in danger of becoming isolated from other animals. Everywhere there are humans and their buildings: other species are hardly visible. What has happened to the age-old arrangement we have with the other animal species to share the surface of this small planet? Has the Animal Contract become obsolete?

We will not survive on our own because we will eventually forget that we are not above natural laws. We may be very clever and we may be able to transform the surface of the earth, but in the end we are no more than humble mammals. We cannot escape the laws of nature and we need the other animals around us to remind us constantly of our true origins and our biological limitations.

One of our greatest losses is the company of working animals. These long-suffering companions have been with us for thousands of years and helped us to build our great nations. It is not exaggerating to say that without them human civilisation could not have developed. We owe everything to them and yet all too often we have treated them not as our partners, protected by a fair Animal Contract, but as our slaves, exploited sometimes beyond endurance.

The story begins about 12,000 years ago, when man and

131

dog entered into the most enduring business partnership of all time. In a Middle Eastern tomb dating from the tenth millenium BC the curled-up skeleton of an old woman has recently been discovered. Her hand is resting on the skeleton of a puppy aged between three and five months. Since we know that the woman came from a culture that did not eat dogs, it would appear that the puppy was kept as a companion, and one that merited special burial with the elderly woman: as early as 9600 BC the domestic dog had arrived on the human scene.

It has always been considered that hunting was the common pursuit that forged the original link between man and dog, but this is unlikely. No dog would co-operate on the hunt unless it had been previously tamed and humanised. In reality the very first relationship was probably that of predator and prey, with man as the predator. Among the young puppies brought home for the pot, some would have been spared as pets for the children or the elderly, growing up with a strong attachment to their human companions and probably coming to act as guard dogs. With their highly sensitive ears and noses, they could detect intruders, especially at night, far better than any human. Barking an alarm, rather than hunting, was likely to have been their primary adult role and one that led to generations of breeding and taming.

At this early stage the 'dog' of prehistoric man was still little more than a domestic wolf. It comes as a shock to most people to be told that our very first animal partner was a wolf in dog's clothing. This is because the image of the big, bad wolf we are given as children is wildly distorted. The wolf is depicted as a creature so savage and bloodthirsty that it is hard for us to accept it as the recent ancestor of the friendly dogs we meet in the street. Yet this is what it is. All modern breeds of dog, from Great Danes to chihuahuas, have descended from this

132

common ancestor in what is genetically a very short period of time, and they still retain most of the wolf's personality and behaviour patterns. The wolf's complex social organisation, its hunting skills, its restrained aggression, its devoted parental care and its highly developed sense of social co-operation and mutual aid, all remain very much a part of the dog's world. Now, however, the mutual aid and co-operation is directed not only at other members of its own species, but also at its adopted human companions.

Anyone doubting that their small lap-dog could possibly be related to the wolf only has to meet a tame wolf to have those doubts swept away. People who keep wolves as pets today soon discover how quickly they become attached to human families. If they differ at all from domestic dogs in personality, it is in that they are slightly more shy of strangers. They are certainly no more aggressive, despite their reputation. Some owners, in order to avoid trouble, have pretended that their pet wolves are Alsatians so as to be able to take them for walks on a collar and lead. One wolf-owner registered his animal as a pet dog when he crossed the Atlantic on a luxury liner and exercised the animal each day on the main decks. Had the other passengers known the truth there might have been panic; instead they patted the 'charming dog' and praised its beautiful appearance.

There is little doubt that, once it had become established as a friend of prehistoric man, the wolf did eventually become a companion on the hunt. Its superior senses of smell and hearing must have been invaluable, and its urge to co-operate with its adopted human pack made it the ideal partner. This additional role exploited the natural hunting behaviour of the wolf pack; from that behaviour different elements were developed by selective breeding to create new breeds of dog.

Each wolf pack spends about one-third of its time hunting, and a great deal of that time is occupied by searching. The wolf travels an average of 24 miles between kills, which immediately gives some idea as to why domestic dogs are so eager for long walks with their owners. During this travelling the wolves are constantly alert for any interesting scents. Their sense of smell is so good that when they do come near a prey they can detect its presence by its odour at distances of up to one-and-a-half miles, providing they are downwind. A more typical distance, however, is about 300 yards.

As soon as the lead animal has detected the odour of a potential prey, it stops suddenly and stays rigid, its eyes, ears and nose all pointing in the direction of the scent it has picked up. This attracts all the other pack members, who follow suit. A curious group ceremony may take place, in which the wolves cluster together, standing nose to nose with their tails wagging, rather like an American football team going into a huddle before an important play. Nobody knows what is happening in this huddle but it leads to a dramatic change of direction of the pack, which now makes off towards the prey.

As they approach the prey, stalking it carefully, the lead animals inevitably arrive sooner than the rest, who are straggling behind. The leaders show self-restraint at this point, lying down on the ground while the others catch up. They do this in the pointing position, still focusing their sense organs on the prey. The stalking takes them up to within 100 or even only 30 feet of the prey. It is their goal to get as close as possible before revealing themselves and going into the attack.

Eventually the prey detects their presence and faces them. They now make a cautious approach, testing the mood of the prey. If it is a large animal that stands its ground or charges them they will probably give up the attack and wander off in search of a weaker challenge. Wolves cannot afford to be brave: an injured wolf quickly starves to death. If the prey panics and starts to flee, then the wolves respond in an instant with a mad rush towards it. If they do not catch it immediately they will chase it for half a mile before giving up. They have been known to keep chasing for as far as three or even five miles, but such marathons are rare. Running for twenty minutes is usually as much as any wolf will attempt, after which it prefers to conserve its energy for use against a less athletic prey.

During both the stalking and the chasing phases of the hunt, the pack often spreads itself out to surround the prey, some wolves moving off to the side while others remain in the central position. This encircling action helps to panic and confuse the prey. Occasionally one or two wolves leave the pack and go far ahead of it to flush the prey towards it. This driving or ambush technique has been exaggerated in some reports, but it undoubtedly does occur, as does the deliberate use of special local features of the landscape. Some packs learn how to drive prey into deep snow where it is slowed down, or to the tips of projecting land where it is cut off by deep water from any further retreat. Far more common, however, is a simple chase until the prey is exhausted and can be brought down.

The kill itself is a messy business, with wolves attacking from all sides, biting, tearing and clinging on to the weakened animal until, suffering from shock and loss of blood, it collapses and is torn to pieces. The wolves then proceed to gorge themselves, burying surplus food that they cannot consume. After they return to their home base they will regurgitate half-digested meat to any animals, such as lactating females or cubs, that have remained behind at the den. This food-sharing is a regular feature of the wolf's highly co-operative social life.

It is easy to see how prehistoric man, setting off to hunt with a few tame wolves tagging along behind, could have made use of the wolf's instinctive responses. It is also clear that many of today's specialised dog breeds have been developed without much difficulty simply by exaggerating one of these hunting elements. For example:

Travelling: The wolf's urge to set off on lengthy journeys made it possible to develop breeds such as the Dalmatian, the specialised coach dog that ran with its master's coach for mile after mile without fatigue.

Scenting: The wolf's long searching for the scent of its prey made possible the development of scent hounds such as the bloodhound. Breeding floppy ears reduced the sound input, enabling these animals to concentrate even more single-mindedly on the scent being pursued.

Pointing: The wolf's response of freezing on detection of a prey scent is perfected in the pointer, a hunting breed that will hold itself rigid for long periods of time if necessary, until its human companion signals it to move on again. Such is their exaggerated specialisation that some pointers have been known to stand rigidly still, like statues, for up to several hours.

Lying down: Wolves lying in ambush or waiting for other pack members to catch up with them often stay quietly sitting in the grass, pointing towards the prey. This action has been developed to a fine art in the breeds known as setters.

Stalking: The cautious approach of the wolves in order to

surround the prey has been developed into the 'rounding-up' behaviour of hard-working sheepdogs and other herding breeds. With them, the tactics of surrounding and driving the 'prey' have come to dominate everything else, so that they never attempt to complete the sequence with an attack on the sheep. Their task is not easy, because the single prey animal has become a whole flock of sheep and the whole pack of wolves has become a single sheepdog. They must therefore work extremely hard to surround the 'prey', rushing this way and that, trying to take up all the positions of the group of encircling wolves.

Chasing: If the prey flees, the wolves set off in hot pursuit, watching it closely as it runs. This is the pattern that has been refined in sight hounds such as the amazingly swift greyhound which is capable of reaching speeds of up to 41 miles per hour.

Killing: When the wolves finally attack the prey they try to hang on with their powerful jaws, often grabbing the animal by its nose, flanks and rump. This is the quality developed in fighting, baiting and massive guard dogs that fearlessly clamp their jaws on to bears, bulls, criminals or rival fighting dogs. Breeds specifically developed for this purpose were bulldogs, mastiffs and bull terriers, each with huge jaw muscles and a bold, tenacious personality.

Flushing: On the special occasions when certain wolves flush out prey and drive them towards the other pack members, their behaviour is of the type developed in driving gun dogs such as spaniels.

Food-sharing: The wolf pattern that involves the bringing back of food to the den to share it by regurgitation with the non-hunters is the basis of the specialisation seen in the retrievers that are developed to bring shot birds and mammals to their owners and hunting partners.

In all these different ways, wolves were gradually differentiated into various kinds of domestic dog. As the centuries passed, more and more specialisations occurred, until today we have over 400 breeds of dog, all of them essentially wolves, but each with a special quality carefully refined and improved by selective breeding. They all began as working partners, each having a particular role: hunting, chasing, guarding, digging, retrieving or scenting. This was genetic engineering on a grand scale, lasting for thousands of years. No other animal has become so versatile in its working relationships with mankind. For their owners they have proved to be perfect partners, unshakably loyal because they see their human companions as members of their packs, easily controlled because they see them as dominant individuals that must be obeyed, and friendly to a fault because they also see them as pseudo-parents who feed and care for them as if they were overgrown puppies.

The terms of the contract we offered the dog were simple: if you will carry out certain tasks for us, we will care for you and feed you. Where the owners have been decent people, the contract has also been a decent one, and the intertwined lives of the humans and the dogs have been mutually fulfilling. Where the owners have been cruel or unfeeling, the contract has been less satisfactory, however, because the dog's trust in its companions has rendered it susceptible to exploitation and maltreatment.

Even where owners have been well meaning, they have often failed to understand the basic needs of their faithful animal friends. As long as working tasks have been essential to the partnership, the dog's great urge to travel and chase and perform intense physical activities has been satisfied, but when those tasks have been taken over by machines, their lives have not always been appropriate or satisfying. A dog bred to race over the fields day after day is not well suited to the easy life of the city apartment. An ex-herding, ex-chasing or ex-gun dog that is given little exercise and no real pack life, has an existence that is far from perfect, however good it may appear to be. Like humans, dogs need group activity and personal challenge. Without it they become impatient, neurotic and restless.

*　　*　　*

Despite appearances, working dogs are generally better off than pampered ones, but the same cannot be said for many beasts of burden. For them the carrying of heavy loads has no natural significance. It fails to trigger any deep-seated biological responses. It is merely a chore, an imposition thrust on them by men who for many centuries have driven far too hard a bargain.

As early man became increasingly settled and started to acquire more elaborate possessions, he needed a more powerful form of transport than could be provided by human backs. Donkeys, camels, horses, yaks, buffaloes, llamas, reindeer and elephants have all been laden with heavy burdens and whipped into transporting them from place to place. Without this help in the early days of civilisation, there would have been no hope of progress. What machines do today, animals did yesterday. They seem so remote now for most of us that we tend to forget the debt we owe them as we ride along in our horseless carriages: for millennia the long-suffering beasts with broad backs were helping us to build the beginnings of commerce, industry and the whole of modern society.

Five thousand years ago the donkey was already staggering along the tracks of ancient Egypt, weighed down with goods and produce. One of the earliest references to it shows that it was paid as a tribute to Egypt from Libya and it may well be that it was there, on the North African coast, that the wild African ass was first tamed and pressed into service. It was in Egypt itself that full domestication was to take place, with the donkey being employed for a variety of important tasks on the early farms. Previously all carrying and shifting of heavy weights had had to be done by human labourers, and the arrival of the donkey as a pack animal transformed their lives, making them approximately ten times more efficient in executing their farming duties. These docile animals carried heavy saddlebags, helped bring in the harvest, pulled the plough, threshed the corn and, in times of war, assisted with the transportation of vital materials. Long before the arrival of the camel they were the all-purpose beasts of burden.

Having originated in the uplands of northern Africa, where grazing was sparse and conditions hazardous, the donkey was an unusually tough species, used to very poor living conditions. This was its undoing. Able to survive on a diet that would ruin a horse, it was capable of withstanding extremely harsh treatment. Had it been more delicate its human partners would have been forced to offer it a more generous contract, but its resilience meant that it could be subjected to the most severe of regimes and still survive.

Its usefulness led to its spread all around the ancient world and eventually all over the globe, wherever there were particularly difficult tasks to perform or difficult terrain to be crossed. Before long it was carrying not only produce but people, often both at the same time. New duties were added, one by one. It became the treadmill animal, walking blindfold in an endless circle to turn the great stones in the mills. It helped with irrigation, turning the primitive equipment that raised the life-giving water. Much later it was to be put to work in factories and down mines, but it was in these early days of farm labour that it made its greatest contribution. The increased efficiency that it brought to primitive farming was partly responsible for the revolution in food production that led to the formation of urban centres and eventually to civilisation itself.

Given the importance of its role, it is extraordinary that the donkey has been so despised and degraded. The horse was noble, the bull all-powerful, but the donkey was a stupid ass. Instead of being immensely thankful to these tireless load-bearers, we markedly failed to demonstrate such feelings. We should have honoured the donkey, but instead we made it a figure of fun. The reason was that it was simply too patient, too long-suffering, and too easy to keep, with its modest diet and few demands. This made it the perfect beast of the poor. Compared with the lively, prancing, high-spirited horse, it was too placid and suffered the consequences.

We offered the donkey the harshest of Animal Contracts and it remains harsh to this day in those parts of the world where animal power has yet to be replaced with machine power. Often working in temperatures hot enough to fry an egg, these silent servants still live out their long, monotonous lives with an expression that suggests they are merely waiting for death.

Each beast of burden had its own special contribution to

bring to the early development of human civilisation. The donkey brought slow, stolid mobility, but it had one serious drawback: it had very small feet. This may seem trivial, but a great deal of land in the Middle East, where civilisation was beginning, was desert with soft sand. There the donkey was at a grave disadvantage. To make the vital desert journeys a new partner was needed, one with big, flat feet that could cross the sandy surfaces with ease: the camel.

To the tourist visiting the pyramids today, the camel is an essential part of the scenery and yet this great ship of the desert was nowhere to be seen in ancient Egypt. There was no word for it in the Egyptian language and it did not arrive there until the Graeco-Roman period, when Egyptian civilisation was already thousands of years old. Unlike the donkey it was not considered a suitable form of domestic livestock. This is surprising because it had been successfully domesticated for many centuries in the nearby desert lands, where nomadic Arabs made great use of its ability to move across seemingly impossible terrain. Its complete absence from early Egypt was thought by some to be the result of a special taboo, but it now seems more likely that the Egyptians, who were expert animal handlers, simply considered it to be a bad investment. There were several reasons for this. The fertile Nile basin provided lush pastures and these do not suit the camel's peculiar constitution. In a rich environment, camels do not thrive and are liable to succumb to a variety of serious diseases. They are also said to disturb other livestock, perhaps because of their strong odour, and this would not have suited the Egyptians with their well-stocked farms. Camels are large, cumbersome and notoriously difficult to train, and the males can become dangerous at times. Furthermore it is a species that breeds only very slowly.

These considerations ruled out the camel as a beast of burden along the ancient Nile and it was only later, when the whole region was becoming more arid, that it finally infiltrated that part of the world. Elsewhere it had been long established as the ideal animal companion for nomadic tribes. First domesticated in southern Arabia about 5000 years ago, it quickly became the vehicle of their mobility and the mainstay of human society in those hostile desert lands. It was not only a carrier and a steed, but also a supplier of meat, milk and cloth. Even the dung was utilised as fuel. It could carry loads and people long distances, spreading human influence at a rate hitherto unknown. Exchanges of goods and ideas could develop, and markets could grow and flourish. The camel caravans led to nomadic expansion on an unprecedented scale. Commerce and trading were born.

The strange dislike that other domestic animals have for camels was employed to advantage in early battles. This role was discovered by accident when the ancient Persians, seeing a superior number of horses being lined up against them, decided to augment their own forces with mounted camels. Orders were given that all the pack camels should be unloaded of baggage and saddled-up for riders. The result was a spectacular rout, with the enemy's horses turning in panic and fleeing as soon as they came close to the camels. Whether it was the sight of their huge bodies or their pungent smell that caused this effect is not known, but the camel was certainly a useful secret weapon in early warfare. It also had another advantage, for if the war-horses could be persuaded to overcome their fear and pursue the camels, the big-footed desert beasts had only to make for a sandy surface and they were safe. The hooves of the horses quickly floundered in the soft ground and the camels sped away into the distance. It was this that led to certain military leaders of the ancient civilisations employing regular camel-troops. With these they could chase marauding Arabs back into their own territories and defeat them. So it was that camels gradually became incorporated into more and more regions.

As well as the size of its feet, the camel also has the great advantage of being able to travel long distances without water. Reliable records exist of camels making desert crossings with distances of over 300 miles between water-holes. Their owners were grateful for this, but often puzzled over how the animals managed it. Many assumed that the camel must have some kind of water-storage tank inside the body, but this is not the case. It is indeed capable of drinking a huge amount of water in one session – up to one-third of its whole body weight – but this liquid is then absorbed into the tissues in the normal way. The camel's secret is that it is exceptionally good at avoiding water-loss, even at burning desert temperatures. It does this by allowing its body temperature to rise dramatically during the heat of the day, then fall again in the cool of the night. If it is forced to go without water, it will allow its body temperature to fluctuate by as much as 6°C. In humans this would lead to fever reactions, but the camel is immune. This system greatly reduces demands on water-cooling, and crucial amounts of liquid are saved as a result. In addition, the camel's kidney is super-efficient at saving water-loss through urine and the animal's body is capable of withstanding dehydration of over a quarter of its body weight – twice as much as other mammals. No wonder this remarkable animal has been so widely used by desert peoples across the world.

Working camels are still a common sight in many areas. There are about 14 million of them in service, not only in the desert regions but also in towns and cities, where they plod patiently along in the midst of busy traffic. This hardy beast remains an important animal partner in a wide variety of human tasks. Where great pulling strength is needed, however, a different kind of beast is required. In some parts of the world heavyweight bovines were originally conscripted for the work of pulling the plough. Ancient artefacts show that this began thousands of years ago and, despite the coming of the modern tractor, cattle are still employed to pull and drag heavy weights in many countries.

Man and animal were interdependent, sharing the toil equally (as they still do in those parts of the world where machinery has not taken over). It was not a master–slave relationship, but one of equality of drudgery. Such beasts of burden helped to transform the landscape. As human leaders became more ambitious, their new imaginings could be made real by the muscle power of their animals. Palaces could be erected, defences built, streets laid out, and – most important of all for the developing agriculture – more sophisticated irrigation schemes could be introduced. With their powerful animal companions these new leaders could more easily tame the land. Small tribes could swell and grow to become nations. For the animals this meant incessant labour and little rest as they worked to help build the ancient civilisations.

Unlike the heavy-bodied cattle, the elephant's use as a working animal is almost at an end and its wild populations in both Africa and Asia are shrinking fast. Despite Hannibal's brave example in the Punic Wars, the African species has not been worked for centuries and the use of the Asian elephant has become increasingly restricted.

The elephant made a huge impact on the battlefield when seen by the enemy for the first time. Rival armies could be scattered merely by the terror caused by the sight of these armour-plated giants, with swords tied to their trunks and poison-tipped daggers attached to the ends of their tusks. However, it was soon discovered that elephants hated loud noises and that by creating an immense din it was possible to make them turn and flee in panic, flattening their own army in the process.

The elephant's success as a working partner was not much greater and it is now only employed in small numbers by the timber industries in certain parts of the Far East, and for ceremonial purposes. As a beast of burden it has never been particularly efficient, its maximum load being about 600 pounds. As a pack animal it could therefore only do the work of about eight men, making it hardly worth the trouble it took to capture, train and maintain. As a haulier, however, it excelled, being able to transport a log weighing up to two tons. A pair of elephants working together was capable of pulling a load of wood weighing up to five tons. They could also fell large trees simply by pressing against them.

The main disadvantage of the elephant was that it was not economical to breed: it took too long to become adult. Working elephants had to be caught from the wild and this was no easy matter. It involved either building large stockades into which a herd could be driven or applying some other dangerous strategy. Lassoing was attempted, but it was fraught with risks of serious injury, both to man and animal. Drugged bait was tried, using opium to reduce the elephants to a state of sleepy docility, but this required so much of the drug that it was not an economic proposition and, in any case, drugged elephants frequently wandered far away before collapsing and could not easily be found. Pitfalls were dug, but these often injured the elephants which were then useless as domestic stock. In the end, the stockade remained the favoured technique, although this involved huge numbers of men to drive the herd into the trap.

Once caught, a wild elephant had to be tamed and this too was a hazardous, difficult business. Because of its immense power, the humans involved had to establish their dominance in a reliable way. This was usually done by beating the elephant into submission and using sharp-pointed goads to control it. From the earliest days, this led to a basic discovery about elephants: they really do have good memories. They do not forget the individuals who treat them badly and eventually, one day, they casually crush them to death. A special strategy is called for. It is vividly recorded in a fourteenth-century document: a man dressed in a bright colour thrashes and starves the elephant for a week; then another man dressed in a different colour arrives, pretends to attack and drive away the first man, and then strokes and caresses the elephant, bringing it food and water and making a great fuss of it. After fifteen days of this loving treatment, the elephant's human friend gently attaches it to another, fully tamed elephant and takes the two of them off to bathe. Within twenty days the wild animal is ready to be taught and the taming process can be completed.

Human deceit is too much for the intelligence of the average elephant and the grateful giant will remain docile towards its new-found companion and defender. Herein lies another of the shortcomings of the elephant as a domestic animal: not only does each one have to be wild-caught, but it must always be controlled by its own personal handler, or mahout. Any other human will be rejected. It is an extraordinary partnership. To watch man and elephant together is to witness not so much a business relationship as an emotional bond. Almost

147

like a marriage, it lasts for a lifetime, the lifespan of man and elephant being roughly the same. Each handler is faithful to one elephant, and each elephant faithful to one man. It is one of the most remarkable relationships between man and beast.

Working elephants are rarely seen now, but on ceremonial occasions in India they do retain one rather more decorative duty in parades and festivities. They act as a living canvas on which local artists can express themselves, creating a picture to brighten the lives of the onlookers as well as a reminder of the days when body decoration was the principal form of aesthetic expression for our early ancestors. This may appear to be an exploitation of the giant animal, but in reality it is a kind of reverence. The markings are not those of a circus clown, but the trappings of respect, reflecting not ridicule but admiration. Even here, though, the elephant's days are numbered.

The mighty elephant, a shy, retiring, docile animal, has proved to be something of a liability as a working partner. Sadly, as a result, it will soon become extinct. A century from now our descendants will look back on it and wonder what it was really like, just as we look back on the mammoths that were exterminated 11,000 years ago and regret their passing.

*   *   *

The horse was domesticated only relatively recently, but happily it seems to be safe for the future, bred and protected all around the world. Unlike the elephant, its captive breeding causes no problems and it still retains many working roles that we are loath to replace with modern machinery.

The secret of the horse's success as a business partner with mankind lies in its unique combination of strength and speed. Bulls were immensely powerful and we were able to employ them, before the coming of the horse, to do much of our heavy work, pulling the plough and dragging cumbersome carts, but they could not travel fast or cover impressive distances. Dogs, on the other hand, were fast, but even a whole team could pull only a modest weight behind it and then only over smooth surfaces. The horse, once it had been mastered, was capable of carrying both men and materials rapidly over vast areas of land. Speed was the great gift that the horse brought to mankind.

On horseback men could spread and conquer the whole of the planet's land mass. At first pulled in carts, carriages and chariots, and later riding astride a steed's galloping back, the horsemen of the ancient world sped across the surface of the earth. Man's greatest animal slave had arrived, giving mobility on a previously unimaginable scale. The horse was to become no less than the vehicle of the expansion of human civilisation. Sadly it was also to become the deadly vehicle for the escalation of human slaughter. For the warrior it offered an advantage beyond price: from the safety of his mount, the archer could turn and deliver a lethal arrow.

The horse could cover almost any terrain, could ford rivers, climb hills and gallop for miles. Co-operative to a fault, sensitive to command and unflagging in its athletic energy, the horse was the near-perfect companion. From our point of view its domestication was one of the best Animal Contracts that mankind ever made.

For the horse, however, the terms of the contract became more and more severe. As weapons became more sophisticated, the battlefields were soon awash with equine blood. The horse was vulnerable to spears and swords, but when guns and bombs were added to the human arsenal it was entirely defenceless. More than a million horses were shipped from all over the world to take part in the battles of the First World War; few of them were ever to see their native soil again. The slaughter was on a scale difficult to conceive. In a single day's fighting in one of the battles 7000 horses were slain. Bombs and shells simply blew them to pieces. For those lucky enough to survive to the end of the war, there were no medals. Most of them were fed to prisoners of war or sold to French butchers for meat or to continental farmers to be killed and converted into fertilisers. So many were disposed of in this way that the British government profited from their sale to the tune of £5,316, 138, making the British love of horses ring rather false. This was not altogether new. In Elizabethan times it had been said that England was 'the paradise of women, the purgatory of men and the hell of horses'.

Matters finally improved when it became clear that horses were no longer a match for the more advanced weapons devised by human ingenuity. They were eventually excused duty at the front. There was one last attempt to employ them, at the start of the Second World War, when the Polish cavalry valiantly rode into battle against the Germans: they were totally obliterated by tanks and dive-bombers in what must have been the most uneven contest in the history of warfare. That was the end of the horse's long ordeal in the battlefield.

Only when the horse became obsolete did we change our attitude towards it. In the half-century since its last ill-fated charge into battle, its military role has become a symbolic one. Today war-horses perform only ceremonial duties. Patient partners in elaborate human ritual, they are pampered and groomed as never before. Like the elephants, they are lovingly decorated; not, however, with brightly painted colours, but with the gleaming brass and shining leather of the military parade. More respected now than at any time in its history, the horse's contract has been rewritten. It has become a high-status animal, the most noble of beasts and a joy to ride and watch. It is a good time to be a horse. It may still have to work for a living, but the wages are excellent.

Our obsession with the horse is perhaps more intense than with any of our other working animals. For many people it begins in infancy, when even the tiniest of children sit earnestly on the backs of their ponies to develop their riding skills. To sit on a horse is almost to become another animal, a centaur whose head is elevated above the crowd: the riders discover a new, more dominant perspective. The reward of this particular partnership for humans is both physical, with dramatically increased mobility, and psychological. The tight bond that was forged between horse and rider, thousands of years ago, is very much alive.

The softening of our relationship with the horse extends beyond the military sphere and covers the whole range of our involvement with the animal. It is ironic that the harshness that was threatening the great bond that originally existed between us was stripped away by the machine age and the coming of engines. The industrial revolution removed the need to exploit animal labour. The economic imperative ceased and many working animals were made redundant. A nostalgia clause was written into the Animal Contract. The working horse became a quaint reminder of an earlier epoch which we think of today as more graceful and gentlemanly. It was not the epoch itself that was graceful. If there was grace and gentleness it lay more with the horses than the humans: we flatter ourselves if we imagine that their natural elegance rubbed off on the conduct of our ancestors.

This equine elegance may be found in nostalgic celebrations, such as at country fairs, where magically decorated teams of great horses can still be seen. In Britain there is one coach-and-ten including in its number the world's largest horse, weighing over a ton and standing eight feet tall to the top of its head. These and other heavy horses are often decked out in their ornate trappings, the reflection of the sun glinting on highly polished horse brasses. These brasses are more than decoration. Their function is supernatural: they are intended to protect the animals from the evil eye. Some, like the simple sunflash discs, usually worn on the centre of the forehead, dazzle the evil eye so that it cannot see its intended victim clearly. Others, such as the horns and crescent moons, are symbols of protective pagan gods, displayed in opposition to the powers of darkness. These pagan displays are common throughout Europe wherever working horses are shown on ceremonial occasions, and have survived the domination of European communities by Christian beliefs in a remarkably tenacious way. Their success, however, is probably due more to lack of understanding of their true significance than to religious tolerance.

The power of the heaviest of the horse breeds is astonishing. Originally bred to support the weight of knights in armour, these gentle giants were later to become the great draught horses of agriculture. Until about only 50 years ago they were the farmer's main source of field power. Now they are rare reminders of the pre-machine age, beautifully cared for and proudly displayed on special occasions.

At first people were frightened by the new-fangled engines which were to replace the working horse. Their inventor, James Watt, tried to make them more friendly by measuring their strength in a unit he called horsepower, still used today.

Gradually the mechanical devices became accepted and working animals fell out of favour. For those people who lived through this transition from horsedrawn to horseless carriages, the changes must have been startling. The difference between the horsy bustle of the city streets, with the busy clatter of hooves and the gentle aroma of horse dung, and the mechanical grinding of the earliest engines with their pungent fumes was dramatic. It was the sudden dawning of a new age.

The mechanical beasts of burden had one great advantage: they had no feelings. With no nerve-endings and no emotions, they could not suffer as working animals had done. Animal pain in the streets vanished, but something else vanished too: our intimacy with the animal world. Animal suffering may have disappeared, but so had animal warmth. The cold, headlamp eyes of the new beasts of burden showed no expression. Only where the skills of the working animals were difficult to replace did the age-old partnerships survive.

*   *   *

Although most working partnerships with animals have been rendered obsolete, with machines able to carry out the old tasks far more efficiently, there still remain certain areas where there are special duties most easily performed by animal companions. There is no risk of the animals being ousted from these tasks, but there does remain the danger of their being exploited and overworked, like so many of their predecessors.

Of all the working species, the one that remains the most versatile and the most valuable is undoubtedly the one with which we have had the longest relationship of all: the dog.

Dogs have performed many varied tasks for us over the centuries. Some of these are now continued only to keep old traditions alive, but there are several important contracts they fulfil because there is no modern substitute for their unique talents. Among these canine partners are guide dogs for the blind, hearing dogs for the deaf, mountain rescue dogs, drug-sniffing dogs and bloodhounds. In each case the dogs accept human hospitality – warmth, comfort, regular food, medical care and social companionship – in exchange for the performance of these special duties. These contracts are not sentimental or nostalgic, and it is hard to imagine that they will ever be superseded.

The herding of farm animals is almost impossible to mechanise. It takes an animal cunning to control other animals on the move. The sheepdog is with us still. This hard-working animal may give the impression of being exploited, but nothing could be further from the truth. Everything it does is derived from its wolf ancestry: its circling of the flock of sheep as though it were a whole pack of wolves; the crouching and waiting; the constant response to the changing moods of the leader of its pack, the shepherd – all of these are wolf-like qualities. Only the kill is inhibited. The rest is natural hunting behaviour, converted and transformed into a valuable dog–man partnership. The hard life of the sheepdog is full of challenge and incident, of novelty and complexity. It is ideal for the canine personality. With a kindly shepherd the sheepdog is in something approaching a canine paradise, with all its urges fulfilled daily in an ideal Animal Contract. Since there is simply no other way of herding sheep, the sheepdog's role is safe for the time being.

In Australia the rounding-up of cattle used to be an exclusively animal duty, with the stockmen's horses and dogs playing their vital part. It seemed this would always be so, but then the local farmers became rich enough to buy helicopters to carry out the task. The traditional stockmen became flying cowboys who drove their cattle along by terrorising them from the air. It was claimed that this would prove to be a more efficient and speedy way of moving the cattle, despite the initial cost of the machines. However, certain farmers found this attempt to modernise the ancient task of driving cattle panicked the animals. It caused such stress that they began to lose weight. Their poor condition persisted and the helicopters were abandoned. When the horses returned to their old duties, peace reigned once more and the cattle flourished. When we see an Australian cattleman in action today, we are not looking at a piece of nostalgia: the use of the horse makes good economic sense. In less advanced countries the use of working animals might be a matter of simple necessity, local poverty preventing the purchase of expensive modern machinery; in the Australian situation it is a calculated preference based on the careful correction of an error of judgement.

In our eagerness to progress we often make mistakes of this kind. We are curious, inquisitive little apes, always inventing something new. Occasionally the age-old methods turn out to be the best.

One context in which human ingenuity has failed to match the dog's natural skills is drug detection. To witness a drug-sniffing dog in action is rather like watching a master magician performing an impossible trick. In a typical demonstration, cannabis is placed in a thick cellophane packet which is sealed tight. This is then enclosed in a parcel and the parcel placed in a box. The box is sealed and placed inside a canvas mail bag, which is thrown into the middle of a pile of 40–50 such bags.

Will the drug-sniffing dog be able to locate it? Common sense insists that it will not, but the nose of a dog contains an uncommon sense and, despite the almost unimaginable weakness of the triple-wrapped scent signal from the drug, its fragrance is rapidly detected and the animal eagerly grabs the bag in question, shaking it like a rat, and tugging at it in excited triumph. There is no scientific equipment that could even approach this feat of detection and there is certainly nothing nostalgic about this Animal Contract. It involves a real task very much of the present day. Furthermore, the excitement the animal shows at a successful detection underlines that this is in no way a corruption of canine behaviour, but rather a celebration of it. The working dogs in this case may be servants of man, but they live a fulfilled, rewarding life.

The rewards for their handlers are also great. Many millions of pounds' worth of narcotics have been found and destroyed as a result of their dogs' activities. One mongrel alone has made 160 separate finds of hidden drugs – a total of 4040 kilos, worth more than £4 million. This particular animal, a labrador cross, was capable of detecting narcotics through steel doors, inside bibles, submerged in bath salts, sealed in tin cans, and – most astonishing of all – in sellotaped plastic bags submerged in coolant fluid. The cunning of the drug barons is no match for the canine nasal tissues.

In all these animal partnerships, where animals are acting as our servants, it is hard to be certain how fair the contracts are. It is easy to tell when an animal is in pain, but much more difficult to tell whether or not it is being unfairly exploited. Any lifestyle that utilises natural behaviour and develops it is bound to provide a fulfilling existence for the animal concerned. If the animal is lively, active and healthy, and is being asked to perform a duty that uses its special qualities as a species, then who is to say that it is being demeaned by its labour? The line between fair employment and unfair exploitation is a difficult one to draw.

*   *   *

Animal partnerships still flourish in the world of sport, where the horse continues to hold its place, not as a token but as a major figure. Here the animal is still preferred by the vast majority to the machine. For all the popularity of motor racing and speedway, the horse remains the most successful and the most attractive sporting vehicle available to man or woman: the beauty of thoroughbred horses in full gallop is unbeatable.

Racehorses are the most highly prized of all animals: one young animal recently fetched a staggering $13 million at auction. In this context our old companion the horse has become big business. These are star animals and they enjoy star contracts but, as with many human stars, their lifestyle leaves something to be desired. They may lead pampered lives, but the terms of their contract are anything but lenient.

Inbred for generations to create the supreme muscular frame, the thoroughbred has almost reached the limit of its athletic ability. Its success is now largely a matter of how relentlessly the great pump of its heart can keep pounding away, beat after beat. During a race the horse gallops at speeds of between 30 and 40 miles per hour, and its heart can speed up by as much as ten times, from a mere 25 beats a minute to a staggering 250 beats. Overraced, the horse easily succumbs to an enlarged heart and serious health risks.

In order to keep them ready for a sudden explosion of muscular energy when the race-traps fly open at the start of an important race, they are kept shut up for most of their lives in small stalls, isolated from others of their kind and allowed little chance of free exercise. When exercise is given it is carefully controlled and strictly limited: the racehorse must never waste an ounce of energy that could take it past the winning post a fraction of a second faster than its rivals. The racehorse's world is a highly artificial one, but there are compensations, not least being the immense care that is taken over the animal's physical condition and comfort.

There are some who would argue that all horse-racing is an exploitation of the animals involved and should be abolished. They claim that professional racing is based on human greed and pride and that the horses are merely brainwashed accessories. The most severe critics believe that these supposedly cosseted creatures are in reality 'bred and fed to a point of madness and driven to race often to death'. It would be hard to find a lunatic horse and it is a wild exaggeration to suggest that they are 'often' raced to their deaths. There are occasional deaths, it is true, but their frequency is such that a modern racehorse is no more likely to lose its life on a particular day than, say, a wild zebra. Such criticisms usually seem to reflect more a distaste for big business than a concern for the true condition of the animals involved.

Some attacks, however, are more justified. The demand that whips should be abolished in all races is difficult to fault. If some horses need pain to encourage them to win races, they should lose them: in no time at all such animals would vanish from the racetracks, as failures. Only horses that genuinely enjoyed racing and needed no more than the jockey's voice and body language as encouragement would succeed. The permitted use of the whip is a clause that could with advantage be removed from the racehorse's contract.

A separate attack on the racing world is an intriguing one. It has been argued that, since it is against the law to ill-treat animals, it is irrational that we can 'give them the ultimate ill-treatment of death without a vet's certificate recommending euthanasia'. If the racing world really cares about its animals, then why do so many owners have their horses (or greyhounds) killed as soon as their usefulness on the track is over? Many people do not realise that this is normal practice for the majority of racing animals, and it certainly reduces the impact of the emotional defence of racing made by its proponents. The introduction of a regulation that a registered racing animal may not be killed if it is healthy, regardless of its age, would separate the callous, greedy owners from the genuine horse-lovers (or greyhound-lovers) and would help to restructure the racing world in a manner that would greatly improve its image. There is already a minority of owners of racing animals who are at pains to reward them with a comfortable retirement after their racing days are over, so that this suggestion is certainly not demanding the impossible.

It is strange that the racing world does not wish to put its own house in order without outside interference, but it must be remembered that it is a sphere of human activity that still drags one boot in the mud of earlier hunting days, when Animal Contracts were far more brutal. With the rapidly changing climate of social opinion concerning the treatment of animals, only the most blinkered of administrators in racing circles can be unaware of the risks they are running. It would be a serious loss if public opinion turned against the racing world, for it would mean the removal of yet another vital link between the human and animal world. It is designed to be a benign link, with no harm intended to the animals. In theory it is a celebration of the beauty and speed of the creatures concerned. If the abuses mentioned are eliminated then it will also, in practice, be a genuine honouring of magnificent animals and our bonds with them. To abolish racing would mean their extermination and the elimination of their persuasive influence on our appreciation of supreme animal qualities.

Fortunately the understanding between horse, rider, trainer and owner is usually sufficiently sensitive for the future of this most stylish of animal partnerships to be secure. With the abuses removed we will be able to continue to marvel at this extraordinary beast, that quietly allows a bipedal ape to become a proud quadruped once again by sitting on its back.

A number of animals have been co-opted into competitive racing, with varying degrees of seriousness. In East Africa and the Caribbean, there are regular hermit-crab races. The animals are land-crabs found near the shoreline and given special colours or numbers by painting their shells. They are placed under an inverted basket on the centre of a smooth, circular floor and, after all bets have been placed, the basket is swiftly lifted by an overhead string and the race begins. The first crab to reach the rim of the floor is the winner. They are then caught up, replaced in the basket and betting can begin for the second race.

The problem with crabs is that they move in a crab-like way, often walking sideways in a continuing curve that takes them right up to the edge of the floor and then away from it again, much to the anguish of the punters. This adds an element of uncertainty to the race which heightens the excitement. The reason why the crabs move so fast during these events is that they dislike open spaces and, as soon as the basket is removed, they set off in search of some other protective cover. The open floor offers no such protection so they simply keep on going until they escape from its bleakness. An additional element of uncertainty exists in the form of their more extreme reaction to finding themselves suddenly in an open space, namely to retract inside their shells and hide. The crab that ran fastest in the first race may well be the one that was most upset by the open space. There is therefore a good chance that this will be the one which, faced with a second race, decides enough is enough and gives the stronger reaction of hiding in its shell and remaining completely immobile. It is not safe to play the favourites with hermit-crabs.

These uncertainties and the simplicity of setting up the racetrack have made crab-racing an appealing if modest pastime; other forms of animal racing are more elaborate. Camel-racing in Arabia can become an intensely serious sport with specially imported child jockeys and a phalanx of Land-Rovered sheiks following the galloping animals as they strike out down the racetrack. In Lapland, reindeer ski-racing is far less intense, but extremely hazardous for the skiers, whose long reins frequently become tangled up as the unruly deer criss-cross one another's paths. If there is any cruelty here it is self-inflicted by the human competitors on themselves.

Pigeon-racing is a curious phenomenon since with every contest it gives the birds complete freedom to abandon their Animal Contract and fly off to any location they wish. There is no physical restraint, but this is replaced by considerable psychological pressure. The pigeons, with their amazing homing abilities – involving the use of clues from the sun, the stars, the visual landscape, the sound landscape and the earth's magnetic field – are keen to fly to the home loft for sexual reasons. Their owners ensure that their birds are well paired and rely on the fact that, when separated from their mates, they will feel a powerful urge to be reunited. The simplest system permits the racing of both cocks and hens, each of them wishing to return to their shared nest-site. A more manipulative system allows only the cocks to be raced. This requires careful stage-management of the lovelife of the pigeons, with the male being kept from his female until just before the race when he is permitted access to her. Before he can satisfy his avian lust he is whisked away, popped in a basket, and carried off to the start of the race. Needless to say he hurries home so fast that, with luck and favourable winds, he is much more likely to win a large prize for his owner. An even more devious form of sexual frustration is popular in Belgium, the world centre of pigeon-racing. There, the racing male, moments before he is taken away and put in the racing basket, witnesses to his horror his female being placed in the company of another male. His bird brain seething with jealousy, he makes the return journey at the greatest speed of which he is capable.

In general, the terms of the Animal Contracts involved in the staging of races, whether for birds, horses, or any other species, are not too severe. The man–animal partnerships are reasonably fair. Occasionally there are excesses, as with some of the very long-distance sled-dog races and the most demanding of the steeplechases, such as the Grand National. These events go beyond providing a test for the animals and offer them instead an ordeal. For many who witness the National on television, the crashing falls are too much. They come to think of all horse-racing as brutal and disgusting, basing their experience on this one atypical event. In fact, the continued running of the National probably does more harm to the cause of horse-racing than any other single factor. Yet within certain segments of society it remains immensely popular and even those who hate it can still find themselves watching it with morbid fascination, rather as if they are witnessing a motor-way pile-up.

Other sporting partnerships with animals are also less than benign. They nearly always involve horses. Polo, show-jumping and eventing put heavy demands upon the animals con-cerned, but for most people these demands are not too severe. They are spectacles enjoyed by vast numbers of spectators, who witness not only the occasional falls, but also an enor-mous amount of close affection between rider and steed and an almost non-stop demonstration of the harmony that can exist between humans and non-humans – a lesson in planet-sharing that is, perhaps, worth the rare crash when horse or, more likely, rider is hurt.

As a risk-taking species we have always felt the need to take part in mildly dangerous pursuits. If life gets too safe, we find some ingenious way of making it risky again. At our most human we are simply not designed for the quiet life. Serenity soon breeds boredom and boredom breeds discontent. The thrill of a race has special appeal for us: it is a breathless moment of high-risk action for both horse and rider. The spectators can add a further risk to bring the occasion to life by gambling their hard-earned money on the event. Where sport has replaced war and the thoroughbred race has replaced the cavalry charge, the punter has replaced the soldier. His bond with the horses retains its element of danger and surprise.

For some, the need to experience the dangers traditionally involved in the man–horse partnership requires more extreme acts of daring. The rodeo provides these. Originally a Wild West demonstration of cowboy riding and roping skills, it has become a widespread and regular form of animal sporting entertainment in North America, where it arouses strong emotions both in its defence and against it. It is a sport that focuses not on co-operation between man and animal but on brutal competition.

The main rodeo events are bronco-riding, bull-riding, calf-roping and steer-wrestling. In the riding events, the object is to stay on the animal's back for a number of seconds while it kicks and bucks wildly. The spectators are so hypnotised by the undoubted bravery of the riders that they fail to ask themselves why the horse or bull is behaving in such a mad-dened fashion. If they read the official description of rodeo practice they would find the innocent statement that, 'Nobody knows what makes horses buck. In approved rodeos they are not starved, nor tormented, nor stimulated into bucking; they buck for the love of it.' The truth is somewhat different, as a recent campaign against rodeos in the United States has revealed. The campaigners demanded the prevention of 'the use of twisted wire snaffles, bucking straps, electric prods or similar devices, all of which are standard equipment for making animals perform in rodeos'. The favourite device is the bucking or cinch strap which is fastened tightly into the groin, causing painful pressure that produces non-stop bucking of the type demanded for the rodeo spectacle. Some-times caustics are applied to the animal's genitals or rectum to make it writhe even more. Electric goads are useful for making the animal shoot out of the release stall at the drama-tic moment.

When the rodeo was first brought to Britain, back in 1924, and staged at Wembley Stadium, there was an outcry against it. The calf-roping and steer-wrestling were particu-larly disliked and attacked as cowardly displays of pointless

164

brutality. In calf-roping a galloping animal is lassoed, thrown and its legs quickly roped, causing the creature considerable pain. In steer-wrestling, the animal is not roped, but thrown by the cowboy grappling it to the ground. Again, the animal inevitably suffers considerable stress.

The organisers of the Wembley rodeo were promptly prosecuted for cruelty to animals, but it took ten years for full legislation to be introduced to prevent rodeos in Britain. It became an offence to throw an 'untrained bull with ropes or other appliances; to wrestle, fight or struggle with an untrained bull; and to ride or try to ride any horse or bull stimulated by the use of a cruel appliance, such as a cinch rope pulled tight around its genitals'. In North America and Australia, however, the rodeo continues unabated, although it is noticeable that in recent years attempts have been made to conceal the cinch rope as much as possible by ensuring that it is, wherever feasible, the same colour as the coat of the animal it is tormenting.

Defenders of the rodeo still insist that the animals involved do not have such a bad deal. It is, after all, an Animal Contract that only involves at worst (and reluctantly admitting that perhaps they do feel some discomfort when bucking) a few seconds of pain, and the damage to the human partner is potentially much greater. Even if, for the greater part of its life, the rodeo animal is cosseted and cared for, the artificiality of the rodeo drama makes it offensive. These are not really wild or unbroken animals being tamed by courageous stockmen for any serious agricultural purpose. They are docile beasts driven to wildness for our entertainment, exploited by men seeking prize money. This is nostalgia for the long-lost days of the Wild West, but it is nostalgia gone sour. It is a contrived Animal Contract that does us no credit and which only provokes opposition to all forms of working-animal partnerships.

*   *   *

For most city-dwellers, the working animal has become remote, a figure of history, fit only for taking us on romantic rides into a sentimental past. Because modern machinery has made most working animals obsolete, there is a tide of opinion that wishes to put an end to this animal nostalgia. Domestic animals, it is argued, are the equivalent of human slaves. We have abolished human slavery and we should now abolish animal slavery. No matter how benign their slavery may be, no matter how well the animals are treated, they are demeaned by the duties they must perform. Only wild animals, left in peace, are acceptable to this view, which is based on the understanding that we are all animals and that, as our animal relatives, all other creatures should be treated as our equals. All use of animals for human benefit is unjustified.

This is the view of the most extreme followers of the animal liberation movement. At the heart of this creed lies a deep respect for animal life, and in theory it is an ideal philosophy. In practice it has one major flaw: its effect would be to distance human populations from all other species. By maintaining our working relationships with domestic animals, even though they are no longer economically essential, we encourage that close bond of intimacy that lets us know other animals and ensures that we continue to care about them.

Domestic animals cannot be freed like human slaves. They have no wild homes to go to, so that to de-domesticate them would be to destroy them. The swollen human populations have already pushed back the remaining wild animals to a point where for most people they are nearly invisible. We would end up in an animal-free zone of isolated human existence. The animal world would be out of sight, out of mind and before very long, out of space. We need the constant presence of animals as a reminder to us of our animal nature. We are animals, and not gods. We are not above the laws of nature. We must learn to live within those laws: we must learn to share this limited biosphere with the other animals.

Cruel animal partnerships are an abomination, but benign ones are a joy to behold: the world would have a narrower horizon and a bleaker landscape without them. Our fight to protect remote, wild animals is laudable but it is not enough. We need more intimate contact, or our children will eventually become so distanced from all animal life that they will start to view it merely as another exotic fiction flitting across the television screen. Little by little it will disappear until one single species – *Homo sapiens* – smothers the entire earth.

How can we avoid this without perpetuating our old tyranny over our long-suffering animal slaves? The answer is by re-examining the terms of every Animal Contract to make sure that they are as fair as possible. Each clause in each contract must ensure the minimum exploitation, the absence of all unnecessary suffering, and the maximum possibility for expressing the natural behaviour patterns of the species in question. That is what human caring should add up to, in exchange for the work animals do for us, the food they provide for us and the companionship they give us.

We need a new Bill of Rights for animals, ten commandments that will force us to respect our Animal Contracts in all spheres:

1 No animal should be endowed with imaginary qualities of good or evil to satisfy our superstitious beliefs or religious prejudices.

2 No animal should be dominated or degraded to entertain us.

3 No animal should be kept in captivity unless it can be provided with an adequate physical and social environment.

4 No animal should be kept as a companion unless it can adapt easily to the lifestyle of its human owner.

5 No animal species should be driven to extinction by direct persecution or by further increases in the human population.

6 No animal should be made to suffer pain or distress to provide us with sport.

7 No animal should be subjected to physical or mental suffering for unnecessary experimental purposes.

8 No farm animal should be kept in a deprived environment to provide us with food or produce.

9 No animal should be exploited for its fur, its skin, its ivory or for any other luxury product.

10 No working animal should be forced to carry out heavy duties that cause it stress or pain.

This Bill of Rights does not represent a whimsical ideal. It is practical and feasible. It is, however, very far from being implemented around the globe today. It embodies the less extreme ideas of the animal liberation movement. That movement, in its refusal to accept economic arguments for the maltreatment of any animals, is part of a new enlightenment which represents a major step forward in our attitudes towards the welfare and status of animals. If its members can persuade us to adopt the provisions of this Bill of Rights, they will have achieved an important revision of the Animal Contract.

It is dishonourable to break a contract and that is what we have done with our animal friends. They are our relatives and we too are animals. To be brutal to them is to become brutalised in all our dealings, with humans as well as with other species. Any culture that knows sympathy for its animal companions will be a culture that is sensitive and caring in all respects. Any culture that feels a kinship with animals will be a culture that keeps faith with its roots.

If we forget our humble origins we will soon start to imagine that we can do what we like with our little planet. Before too long we will become the new dinosaurs, fossils of some future age.